THEMES TO INSPIRE

2

FOR KS3

Steve Clarke

Although every effort has been made to ensure that website addresses are correct at time of going to press, Hodder Education cannot be held responsible for the content of any website mentioned in this book. It is sometimes possible to find a relocated web page by typing in the address of the home page for a website in the URL window of your browser.

Hachette UK's policy is to use papers that are natural, renewable and recyclable products and made from wood grown in sustainable forests. The logging and manufacturing processes are expected to conform to the environmental regulations of the country of origin.

Orders: please contact Bookpoint Ltd, 130 Milton Park, Abingdon, Oxon OX14 4SB. Telephone: (44) 01235 827720. Fax: (44) 01235 400454. Lines are open 9.00–5.00, Monday to Saturday, with a 24–hour message answering service. Visit our website at www.hoddereducation.co.uk

© Steve Clarke 2012
First published in 2012 by
Hodder Education, an Hachette UK Company,
Carmelite House, 50 Victoria Embankment,
London EC4Y 0DZ

Impression number   6
Year   2016

All rights reserved. Apart from any use permitted under UK copyright law, no part of this publication may be reproduced or transmitted in any form or by any means, electronic or mechanical, including photocopying and recording, or held within any information storage and retrieval system, without permission in writing from the publisher or under licence from the Copyright Licensing Agency Limited. Further details of such licences (for reprographic reproduction) may be obtained from the Copyright Licensing Agency Limited, Saffron House, 6–10 Kirby Street, London EC1N 8TS.

Cover photo: Image of bee on flower © Tomasz Zachariasz /iStockphoto.com
Illustrations by *Barking Dog Art, Peter Lubach, Tony Randell*
Designed in *Minion Regular* by *The Wooden Ark Ltd (Leeds)*
Printed in India

A catalogue record for this title is available from the British Library

ISBN: 978 1444 12208 4

Contents

Section 1

Expressions of faith

1.1	Why do religions have special books?	**4**
1.2	What is worship?	**8**
1.3	How do people celebrate?	**11**
1.4	Why do some people fast?	**14**
1.5	How is life like a journey?	**17**
1.6	How do people celebrate the birth of a baby?	**20**
1.7	Is marriage important?	**23**
1.8	How do people respond to death?	**26**
The big assignment		**30**

Section 2

Beliefs and teachings about meaning and purpose

2.1	Are religion and science in conflict?	**32**
2.2	Where did life come from?	**35**
2.3	What do religious people think about evolution?	**38**
2.4	Are humans special?	**42**
2.5	Is there a purpose to life?	**46**
2.6	What is death?	**50**
2.7	What is the soul?	**52**
2.8	What is reincarnation?	**54**
The big assignment		**56**

Section 3

Ethics and values

3.1	Do humans have rights?	**58**
3.2	Are there religious rights?	**62**
3.3	Why are people punished?	**66**
3.4	What is capital punishment?	**70**
3.5	How can people defend their rights?	**74**
3.6	Do animals have rights?	**78**
3.7	Are we responsible for planet Earth?	**82**
3.8	Are rich people responsible for the poor?	**86**
The big assignment		**90**

Glossary	**92**
Index	**94**
Acknowledgements	**96**

1.1 Why do religions have special books?

Learning objectives

You will ...
- find out about the contents of holy books
- understand why holy books are important to religious people
- understand how religious people show the importance of their holy books
- compare different interpretations of religious texts.

Think about all the different types of books there are.

You might add holy books or sacred texts to this library. Or you could say that the holy books of the world's religions contain examples of all of these genres.

Holy books are sometimes called sacred texts or scriptures.

Holy books are meant to teach their readers. They teach them:

- how to **pray**
- how to **worship**
- **why** we are **here**
- how to be **happy**
- how to **please God**
- how to **live together**
- to **learn** from the **mistakes** of others.

Why are the holy books so important?

Different people have different ideas about how their holy books came about.
- Some religious people believe that their holy book was written by God himself.
- Some believe that their holy book was written by men, but the things they wrote about were told to them directly by God.
- Some believe that their holy book was written by men who were inspired by God and wrote about their experiences of him.
- Some believe that their holy book was written by men who had a deep insight into the meaning and purpose of life.

Do all people of the same religion agree on what their holy book means?

The simple answer is, no. Since not all people of the same religion agree about how their holy book came about, they do not agree about everything it says.

For example, some Christians believe that God told the writers of the Bible what to write, so they believe that everything described in the Bible must have happened exactly as it is told. Others believe the Bible was inspired by God, so they believe that some of what is written may be open to interpretation.

Some religions have books that help them understand their sacred texts. Although they are the works of human beings, some of them have become part of holy scripture.

For example:
- Buddhist teachings are explained in a set of texts called the **Abidharma**.
- Examples of the teachings of Islam are given in sayings and advice from the Prophet Muhammad. They are called the **Hadith**.

Religion		Holy Books
Buddhism		Sutras
Christianity		Bible
Hinduism		Vedas
Islam		Qur'an
Judaism		Torah
Sikhism		Guru Granth Sahib

This young man is reading the **Talmud**. It contains the writings of Jewish teachers, and helps Jews to understand the **Torah**, their central scripture.

How do people show how important their holy book is?

- They call it by a special name.
- They place it higher than themselves.
- They bow before it.
- They avoid touching it with their hands.
- They keep it in a special place, away from everyday objects.
- They try to learn it by heart.
- They kiss it.
- They read it in its original language.
- They keep it as a scroll.
- They write it by hand.
- They use special paper or parchment.
- They chant it rather than read it.
- They appoint a person to look after it.
- They dress it by covering it in special materials.

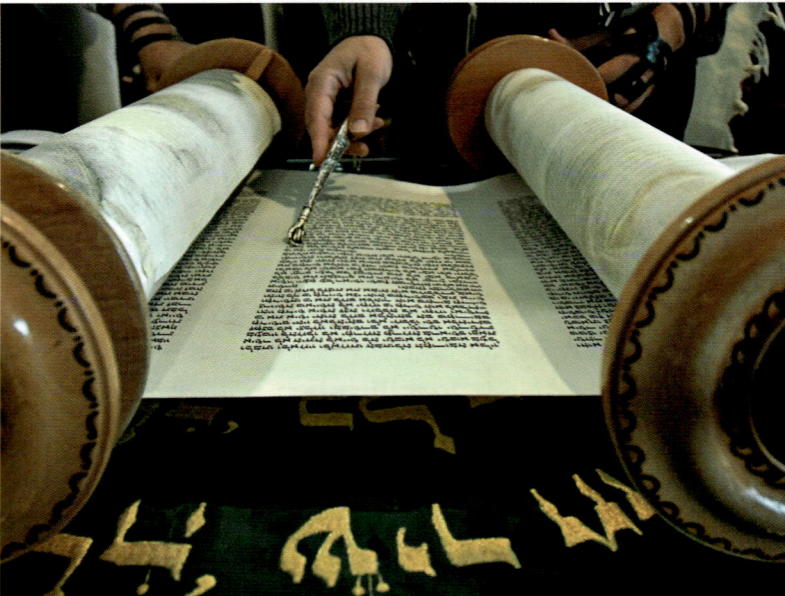

Jewish scriptures are written by hand on scrolls made of parchment. Jews read the scrolls using a pointer called a **yad** so they don't touch it with their fingers.

Muslims treat the **Qur'an** with great respect. It is usually kept in a high place, out of harm's way, wrapped in a cloth. When it is taken down, it is put on a wooden stand to be read from. A Muslim who reads the Qur'an will wash thoroughly first.

Knowledge check

1. What is the main purpose of holy books?
2. What are holy books also known as?
3. Give two examples of the kinds of things holy books teach.
4. Give two examples of how religious people show the importance of their holy book.

Activity A

1. Choose a famous story from the holy book of one religion.
2. Retell it in your own words, and explain why it is important for religious people.

At this Sikh ceremony, the **Guru Granth Sahib** is covered with cloths and carried higher than the worshippers.

Here the **Pope** – the leader of the Roman Catholic Church – kisses a rare copy of the Bible out of respect.

Activity B

1. Conduct some research into the holy books of one religion.
2. Design a cover for the book, illustrating the front with an image of a story, event or theme from the book, and writing some 'blurb' (a paragraph stating what the book is about) on the back.

Activity C

1. Find out about different ways that the holy scriptures of one religion are treated.
2. Find some pictures or videos on the Internet, and put together a PowerPoint® presentation of your findings. Include a slide that explains why they are treated as they are.

Activity D

Many holy books describe supernatural events, like miracles or seeing into the future. Find out about some supernatural events from one religion and how they are interpreted differently by different people. You could present your findings as an illustrated poster.

7

1.2 What is worship?

Learning objectives

You will...
- understand why religious people worship
- know about different ways in which people worship
- compare forms of worship between religions and within the same religion.

What does 'worship' mean?

Worth is how we measure how valuable something is to us. It may be to do with money, but we value things in all sorts of other ways.

Worship refers to the different ways people have of expressing how valuable something or someone is to them. It is how people show respect to something or someone important.

The word 'worship' can be broken down into two parts: *worth* and *shape*. So 'worship' means to shape or form worth, or to make something worthy.

Religions make a distinction between:
- **adoration**, which means worshipping God, and
- **veneration**, which means showing respect to an object or person.

 Buddhists do not believe in God. Most venerate images of the Buddha or representations of some of his characteristics.

 Hindus believe that veneration of images of different gods is an effective way of worshipping God.

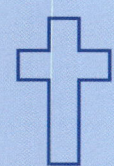 All Christians show adoration to God. Some venerate the bodies of saints, or paintings or statues of them. Other Christians do not practise veneration at all.

 Muslims do not allow veneration in any form. For this reason, mosques do not contain pictures or statues of people or animals.

How do the religions worship?

- singing
- meditation
- prayer
- talks and lectures
- eating
- chanting
- pilgrimage
- playing music
- dancing
- **How do people worship?**
- fasting
- creating works of art
- acting
- studying
- reading
- kissing an object of veneration

9

When they are worshipping, people often try to create a mystical or spiritual atmosphere. They might:
- dim the lights, or burn candles
- burn incense
- dress in special clothes
- be silent.

On the other hand, some people would want to make the atmosphere as lively and joyful as possible. They might:
- decorate the place of worship with bright colours
- make a lot of noise, with musical instruments or their voices
- move around a lot.

Many religious people would say the greatest act of worship is to do good in the world.

Knowledge check

1 What is the literal meaning of the word 'worship'?
2 What are the two main types of worship?
3 Why don't mosques contain pictures of people or animals?
4 Why don't Buddhists practise adoration?
5 Give three examples of how people worship.

Activity A

1 Write a list of some of the things people worship.
2 Describe what they do to show their respect for their object of worship.

Activity B

It is often said that people have five senses: taste, touch, sight, smell and hearing.

1 How do people use their senses in worship?
2 Conduct some research to find some examples of the use of the senses in religious worship.

Activity C

A number of religions use food and drink in worship. Find out how they are used and the reasons behind their use. You could present your findings in a PowerPoint® presentation.

Activity D

1 Investigate different ways of worshipping within the same faith. Try to find out why there is variety and diversity in forms of worship. You could make an illustrated booklet to show what you have discovered.
2 Do you think any one way of worshipping is better than any other? Give reasons for your answer.

1.3 How do people celebrate?

Learning objectives
You will …
- find out about what happens at religious festivals
- understand why people celebrate festivals
- evaluate the importance of celebrating.

Why celebrate?

There are times in the lives of families and communities that have special importance, for example:
- when a baby is born
- when a couple gets married
- when someone passes an exam or gets a new job
- when a new king or queen takes the throne
- when a war ends.

At times like these, people like to be together, in families or communities, to share their happiness with each other.

Most religions have special times when people get together to remember past events or stories, or share their joy at something that has just happened.

Very often people share a special meal together. When this happens, it is called a festival.

People like to celebrate together.

The word 'celebrate' comes from a Latin word, celeber, which means 'a lot of people'.

A celebrity is someone who is admired by a lot of people.

A celebration is an event that is attended by a lot of people.

Knowledge check

Look at pages 11–13.
1. What is a festival?
2. What does Id-ul-Adha commemorate?
3. What do Jews remember at Pesach?
4. What is a Festival of Light?
5. Give two examples of Festivals of Light.

11

Religious celebrations and festivals are always marked by communal acts of worship.
- Wesak is the Buddhist festival associated with important events in the life of the Buddha: his birth, **enlightenment** and death.
- Id-ul-Adha is the Muslim festival that commemorates Prophet Muhammad's willingness to sacrifice his son to Allah.
- Baisakhi is the Sikh festival that recalls the formation of the Sikh brotherhood, the Khalsa.

Christmas is the Christian festival that remembers the birth of Jesus.

Holi is the Hindu festival based on a story of Prince Prahlad and his aunt, Holika.

Festivals of Light

Some religious festivals commemorate stories or events when good overcame evil. Light is very often used as a symbol of goodness, as it can overcome darkness. These festivals are known as Festivals of Light.

Pesach is the Jewish festival when Jews remember their liberation from slavery in Egypt.

Christians believe that Jesus was executed on a Friday (Good Friday), and returned to life three days later. They celebrate this on Easter Sunday. They light a candle, called the **Paschal candle**, which is used throughout **Easter** and lit at other special occasions during the year. It is a symbol of the triumph of life over death, and the glory of Jesus' presence in the world.

For Hindus, **Divali** celebrates the story of the return of Prince Rama and his wife, Sita, to Rama's kingdom after fourteen years of exile. People dress in brightly coloured clothes, spring-clean their houses, and light bright lights to welcome Lakshmi, the goddess of wealth, into their homes.

When Sikhs celebrate Divali, they remember the release from prison of the sixth Guru, Guru Hargobind, and 52 princes. They light up their homes, to symbolise the presence of God; the Golden Temple at Amritsar is filled with light; and fireworks light up the sky. Hymns are sung in Gurdwaras.

Hanukkah is a festival celebrating the re-dedication of the Jewish Temple following victory over the Greeks. They did this by lighting a lamp (**menorah**), a symbol of God's presence. They could only find enough oil to keep the lamp alight for one day, but miraculously it burned for eight days. Jews remember the strength God gave them by lighting a **hanukiah** (an eight-branched menorah). They light a new candle each day for eight days. There is a ninth candle in the middle of a hanukiah that is used to light the other eight.

Activity A

Write your own story of good overcoming evil. How could you celebrate it?

Think about what clothes people may wear; what food they would eat; what music could be played; how light could be used to symbolise aspects of your story.

Activity B

Imagine that you have been invited to spend a day with a religious family at festival time, and you have joined in the celebrations. Write an email to a friend describing the experience. You should include:

- an explanation of why the festival is celebrated
- your thoughts and feelings before the festival
- how the family prepared for the festival
- how the family worshipped during the festival
- what else happened during the day
- your thoughts and feelings at the end of the day's festivities.

Activity C

Why is it important for religious people to celebrate festivals?

Discuss this question with a partner and write a list of your answers. Try to illustrate each answer with at least one example from any religious festival.

Activity D

'People who aren't religious shouldn't take part in religious festivals.'

1. Do you agree with this statement? Support your point of view with reasons and examples.
2. What reasons might someone have for holding a different point of view?

1.4 Why do some people fast?

Learning objectives

You will...
- find out about some religious fasts
- understand why some people fast
- understand why some religions do not accept fasting
- evaluate the benefits of fasting.

Fasting means going without food, and sometimes drink as well, for a period of time. It may seem a strange thing to do, if there are no medical reasons for doing it; but some religions have long traditions of encouraging people to fast.

Fasting is one of the Five Pillars of Islam: it is a religious duty. By fasting, I am showing my obedience to God. It isn't easy, so it teaches me discipline and self-control.

For Christians, fasting can mean giving up anything you desire, but don't necessarily need – like chocolate or smoking. That gives you a chance to reflect on the things that really matter in life.

When I fast, I stop putting myself at the centre of everything. I get rid of ego, and feel at one with all living things.

For me, fasting is a way of getting out of bad habits. We all treat others badly at times, sometimes because it's too much effort to do the right thing. When you fast, you make a big change in your life. It helps you to change other things to make you a better person.

Buddhism

Some Buddhists may choose to fast to prepare them for an important undertaking, but there is no requirement to do so. Before he became the Buddha, Siddhartha Gautama believed he could overcome desire and free himself from suffering by fasting. He came to realise that this was not the way to become truly happy. Instead, he taught moderation in all things: not too much and not too little.

Islam

During **Ramadan**, the ninth month of the Islamic year, Muslims go without food and drink during the hours of daylight. This enables them to think about those people in the world who do not have enough to eat and drink. It helps them to feel their suffering, and encourages them to help the poor and needy.

Christianity

Lent is a period of 40 days leading up to Easter. During this time, Christians remember when Jesus went into the desert and suffered 40 days of hardship in preparation for his work for God. Christians may give up a luxury – something they like but don't need – and spend more time in prayer or study in preparation for Easter.

Sikhism

Some religions do not see the value of fasting, and do not accept it as a religious practice. For example, the Sikh holy book, the Guru Granth Sahib, says:

Fasting, daily rituals, and austere self-discipline – those who keep the practice of these, are rewarded with less than a shell.
(Guru Granth Sahib, page 216)

Judaism

For ten days after the Jewish New Year, Jews try to say sorry to everyone they have been unkind to, and make up with those they have fallen out with. They try to put things right. The tenth day of these Days of Repentance is called **Yom Kippur.** From just before sunset the night before, Jews go without food and drink for the day, while they pray for God to forgive them.

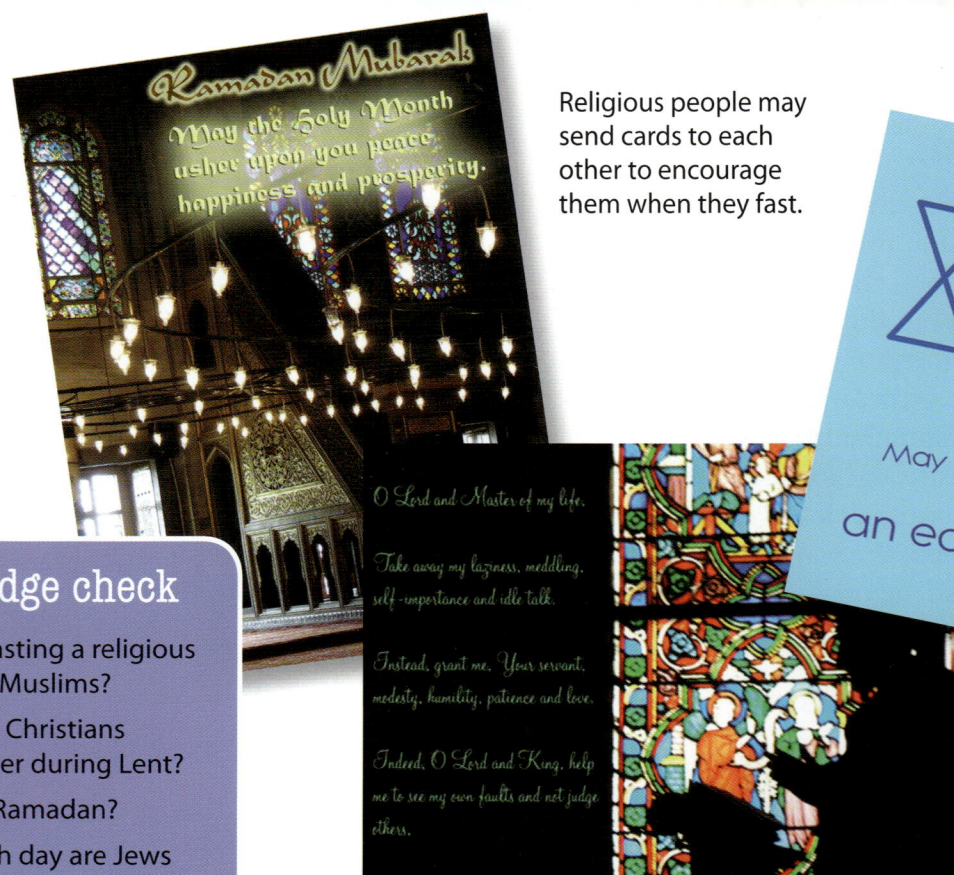

Religious people may send cards to each other to encourage them when they fast.

Knowledge check

1. Why is fasting a religious duty for Muslims?
2. What do Christians remember during Lent?
3. What is Ramadan?
4. On which day are Jews encouraged to fast?
5. Which religion does not accept fasting as a religious practice?

Activity A

1. Think about a time when you have been tested in some way. What happened? What did it feel like?
2. What did you learn from the experience? What good came out of it? What were the negative effects?

Activity B

1. Write an imaginary interview with a Christian, a Jew or a Muslim about fasting. You will need to ask them about when they fast; what religious reasons they have for fasting; what other religious activities happen at the same time; and what benefits they get from fasting.
2. You could write up the interview in a Questions and Answers (Q&A) format.

Activity C

1. Make a booklet about religious fasts.
2. Research teachings about fasting and describe the benefits for those who do it. Try to find quotations from religious writings and holy books to support religious teachings. You may find that people of the same faith may think or do things differently from each other. Try to explain why.

Activity D

1. Do you agree with the Sikh teaching that fasting brings no benefits to those who do it? What reasons might Sikhs have for supporting this view?
2. Why might followers of other faiths disagree?

1.5 How is life like a journey?

Learning objectives

You will ...
- know what rites of passage are
- understand why people celebrate rites of passage
- understand why rites of passage are important for religious people
- analyse how religions mark rites of passage.

How independent are you?

When you were born, you depended entirely on your parents (in all likelihood, your mother) to live.

Now, at your age, you are more independent. You are able to do many things on your own and without your parents' permission. You are responsible for your own behaviour.

When you are an adult, you will be completely independent of your parents.

As an old person, you may start to lose your independence and start to rely on others again – maybe your own children.

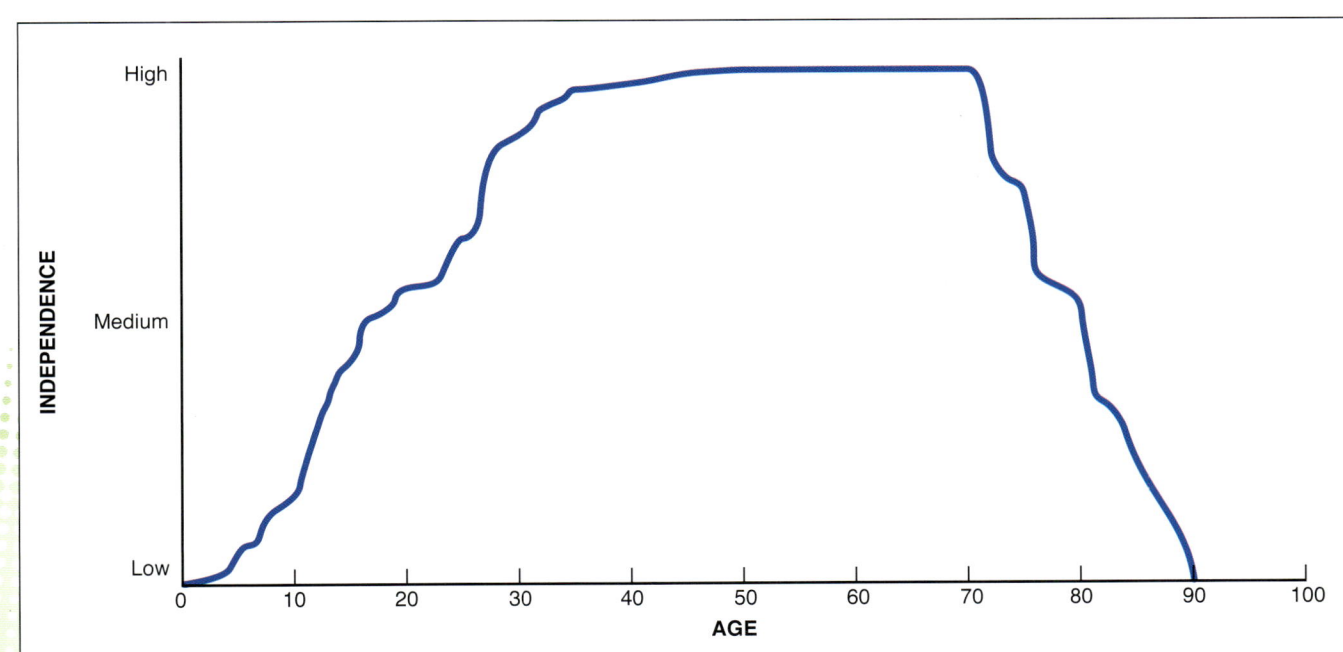

A graph to show periods of independence in a person's life.

The movement from dependence to independence and back to dependence isn't a smooth one. It goes in stages, as you can see from the graph on page 17. Sometimes life is compared to a journey, with the stages like milestones and signposts on the way.

The signs on the map mark stages when changes take place. Often, these stages are marked by celebrations. They are known as **rites of passage**.

Families, communities and societies mark rites of passage: birthdays, passing a driving test, getting married, and many others; they also mark the death of loved ones. At these times, people get together to share their feelings. They dress up for the occasion, and there is usually food, drink and music.

> The word *rite* means *ritual* or *ceremony*. Rites of passage are ceremonies that mark important stages in life as it passes from birth to death.

A pictorial map showing the journey of life.

Rites of passage

Communities and societies have looked to religion to lead rites of passage.

Birth
- It is important for families to welcome someone new, and to give them a name.
- For religions, birth also means new life in the world, and a new member of the faith.

Marriage
- These days, many people set up homes and start families together without getting married.
- Religions see marriage as an important rite of passage, because couples leave their birth families to start new ones, with new responsibilities and greater independence. Religious marriage is seen as a way of gaining God's blessing on a new family.

Death
- All people grieve at the death of a loved one and want to remember them.
- Religions teach that death is not the end of life. Religious people have ceremonies to celebrate the life of someone who has died, mourn their death, and look forward to the continuation of their life in a spiritual form.

Knowledge check
1. What are rites of passage?
2. What is a rite?
3. Name three rites of passage.
4. Why is it important for religious people to celebrate birth?
5. Why is religious marriage important?

Activity A
1. Make a list of important stages in life when changes occur. For each one, say what changes.
2. How is each of these stages marked or celebrated? What happens? Who is involved? Which of them have you taken part in? You could put the information you have gathered onto a poster, and illustrate it; or on a map, like the one on page 18.

Activity B
Some religions mark the stage when a person moves from childhood to adulthood, around the age of twelve or thirteen. At this time, a young person becomes responsible for his or her beliefs, commitments and actions.

Find out about how the start of adulthood is marked in at least two religions.

Activity C
Produce a booklet showing how symbols are used in celebrating or marking rites of passage.

Activity D
'There is no point in marking rites of passage unless you do it with religious ceremonies.'
1. What is your view about this statement? Give reasons and examples to back up your opinion.
2. Why might some people have different views from yours?

1.6 How do people celebrate the birth of a baby?

Learning objectives

You will ...
- understand why religious communities celebrate birth
- learn about some of the things that happen at birth ceremonies
- understand some of the symbolism of birth ceremonies
- compare birth ceremonies from different religious traditions.

The birth of a baby is almost always greeted with joy. It is natural for the baby's parents to want to share their joy with other people. These people are likely to be members of the groups the parents belong to: their families, their friends, their workmates. If they are religious, they will wish to share their happiness with other members of their religious community, so the baby can be welcomed as a new member.

Most religions have ceremonies to celebrate the birth of a baby. They are opportunities to:
- thank God for the gift of new life
- welcome the baby into the world
- welcome the baby into the faith community
- share the joy of the baby's parents
- reflect on the importance of new life
- ask for God's blessings and protection for the baby
- emphasise that the baby's upbringing is a responsibility the community shares with the parents
- give the baby its name.

Many families celebrate the birth of a baby with a religious ceremony.

What happens at a birth ceremony?

Religious ceremonies that celebrate the birth of a new human being vary from religion to religion, and even within the same religion. There are some features that occur in more than one.

Water

Some Christian Churches welcome a baby in a ceremony of **baptism**. In baptism, water is used as a symbol of life, because life cannot exist without water. It also symbolises the Christian belief that God can wipe away a person's evil deeds.

In Sikhism, a baby is given a drop of sugared water (**amrit**) to symbolise eternal life: Sikhs believe that human beings are able to escape life and death to be with God.

Light

Some Hindu families have a special day when they introduce a baby to the world around them. They take it out into the sunlight in the morning, and into the moonlight in the evening.

Christians who baptise babies light candles to represent moving from darkness to light. This is a symbol of the birth itself, and also of God acting in the world.

Haircutting

In Islam, a baby will have its hair cut off. An equivalent weight in gold or silver is given to the poor.

Hindus also shave a baby's head. The hair represents his or her past life, and cutting it off symbolises making a new start.

Circumcision

Jews **circumcise** baby boys when they are eight days old as a sign of the relationship between God and the Jewish people.

Muslims also circumcise baby boys as a religious duty encouraged by Prophet Muhammad.

Prayer

For Muslims, it is important that a baby hears about the greatness of God as soon as it is born. The father, therefore, whispers the **adhan** ('God is great') into the baby's ear so they are the first words it hears.

Hindus use a gold pen dipped in honey to write the sacred syllable, Aum, on a baby's tongue.

Naming

At a Sikh birth ceremony, the Guru Granth Sahib is opened at random. The baby's name should begin with the first letter of the page at which the book is opened.

In Hinduism, a letter of the Sanskrit alphabet is decided by the date and time of the baby's birth. The baby is then given a name starting with that letter.

21

Knowledge check

1. Give three reasons why religious communities like to celebrate birth.
2. What is a Christian birth and naming ceremony called?
3. What is amrit?
4. Why do some Christians light candles when welcoming a baby into their community?
5. When do Jews usually circumcise baby boys?
6. What do Hindus use to write Aum on a baby's tongue?
7. How do Sikhs decide which letter of the alphabet a baby's name should begin with?

Activity A

1. At some religious birth ceremonies, friends and family pray for the future life of the baby. Imagine that, for example, fifteen years from now you have a baby son or daughter. What would you want his or her life to be like? What sorts of opportunities should they take advantage of? What lessons will they need to learn to live happily? What will they have to do to be successful? What would you want the world they grow up in to be like?
2. You could express your ideas in a birth card, or write them as a poem.

Activity B

1. Find out more about birth ceremonies from different religions. What is similar about them? Are there any major differences?
2. Prepare a PowerPoint® presentation to answer the question: Are religious birth ceremonies basically the same?

Activity C

Look again at the reasons why religious groups celebrate the birth of a baby on page 20. For each bullet point, find an example from any religious birth ceremony to illustrate it. If you can find photographs to go with them, you could produce a booklet.

Activity D

'Babies should not have to be part of religious ceremonies, since they are too young to have any religious beliefs.'

1. What reasons might someone have for saying this? Do you agree with it?
2. Why would some people disagree with it?

1.7 Is marriage important?

Learning objectives

You will ...
- analyse statistics showing a drop in the popularity of marriage
- think about why marriage is less popular than in the past
- think about your views on the importance of marriage
- understand why marriage is important in most religious communities
- evaluate the importance of marriage.

How popular is marriage today?

Here are some statistics on the popularity of marriage in Britain:
- Today, there are about 10.6 million married couples.
- About 4 million couples live together without being married.
- Since 1992 there have been more civil marriage ceremonies in the UK than religious ceremonies.

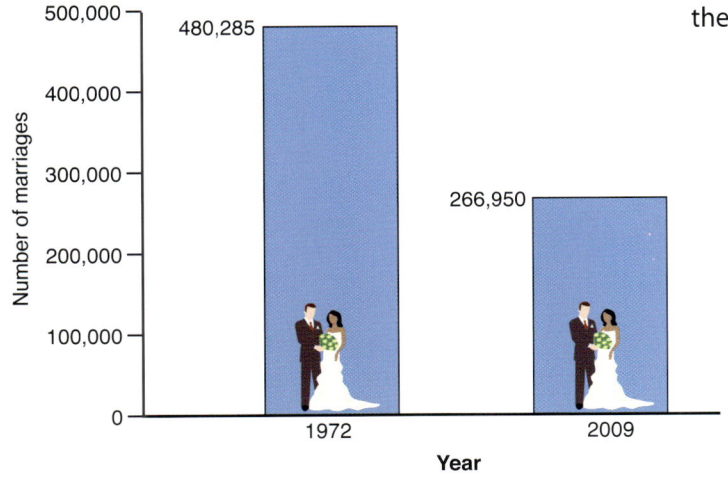

The number of weddings in the UK is declining.

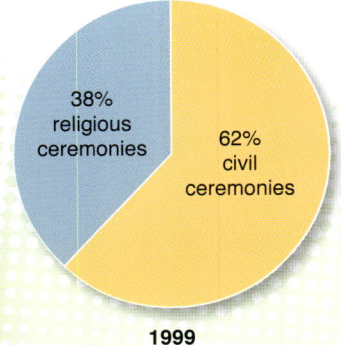

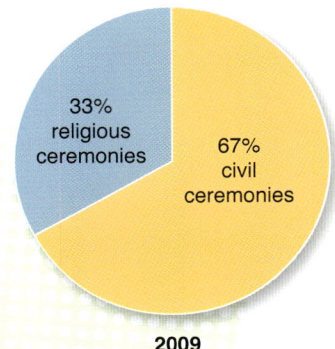

In 2009 civil ceremonies accounted for 67 per cent of all marriage ceremonies, 5 per cent more than in 1999.

Knowledge check

Look at pages 23–25.

1. How many fewer weddings were there in 2009 than in 1972?
2. Roughly, what proportion of couples living together are unmarried?
3. For Christians, what should couples do when they are married that they shouldn't do before they are married?
4. Name two religions that believe in parents arranging marriage partners for their children.
5. In which religion is marriage not considered to be a religious matter?

23

Religions and marriage

Whichever way you look at it, it seems that British people are falling out of love with the idea of marriage. In particular, religious weddings seem to have less importance for them than ever before.

But, for most religions, marriage is still an important institution.

> We love each other and want to spend our lives together. So what's the point of getting married?

Some people think that being married does not change or add to a loving relationship.

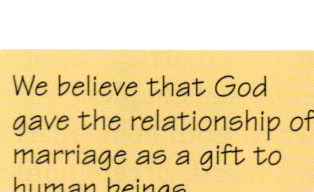

> We believe that God gave the relationship of marriage as a gift to human beings.

For Christians, marriage is the only loving relationship in which it is right to have sex and produce children.

Jews believe that, when they get married, a man and women become one **soul.**

> The Bible says that a human being is not complete until he or she is married.

Activity A

When you are older, would you want to get married, or would you want to live with a partner without being married? Or would you rather be on your own? Discuss these questions with a classmate. Give as many reasons as you can for your answers.

Activity B

1 Research marriage ceremonies from two religions.

2 Make a wedding album showing photographs of various stages of the ceremonies. Underneath each picture, write what is happening and why.

3 At the end, write a paragraph or two to explain what you found interesting about the ceremonies, and whether there were any common themes or ideas.

"We were introduced to each other by our parents. Their decision that we should get married was very wise: we are very happy together."

When a Hindu couple marries, they promise to share food, health, wealth, happiness, children, long life together and truth.

"Getting married means that we are not just partners; we are soulmates."

It is traditional in some Islamic communities for marriages to be arranged by parents.

"We've been together for four years now. We live together, but we aren't married. Maybe we will marry one day."

A Sikh man and his wife are, first and foremost, spiritual partners.

"The Sikh word for marriage means 'blissful union'. Marriage is not just a union of two people: it brings two families together."

For Buddhists, marriage is not a religious matter. Couples tend to do whatever is acceptable in their culture.

Activity C

1. Why do you think the number of people getting married is falling so fast (in this country)? Why are there more civil marriages than religious marriages?
2. Do you think marriage is an important institution? Why (or why not)?

Activity D

1. Do you think that religious people take marriage and family life more seriously than non-religious people?
2. Many religions teach that children should be raised by parents who are married to each other. What reasons do they have for this? Do you agree with them? Why (or why not)?
3. Conduct some research into religious views of family life to provide evidence in support of your answers.

1.8 How do people respond to death?

Learning objectives

You will ...
- learn how religious funerals reflect beliefs about death and life after death
- find out about some symbols associated with death
- compare different funeral rites
- understand how religious practices help people who mourn.

Funerals

When a person's life here on Earth ends, it is marked by a funeral. Apart from disposing of the dead body, the funeral has two main functions:
- to remember and celebrate the life of the person who has died
- to comfort the friends and relatives of the deceased in their grief.

In addition, religious funerals allow people to:
- thank God for the life of the person
- reflect on religious teachings about death and the afterlife
- pray for the deceased's life after death.

Some religions teach that this life is part of a cycle of life, death and **rebirth**. Hinduism, Buddhism and Sikhism are examples. They teach that dead bodies should be cremated, and the ashes scattered on land and in rivers. This ensures that the body connects with the five elements they believe make up our environment: fire, water, earth, air and space.

Some religions teach that, after this life, life carries on in a spiritual way. Judaism and Islam are examples. They teach that dead bodies should be buried. They teach that human beings were created by God from the earth, and they should return to earth when they die.

Christians, like Jews and Muslims, have a tradition of burying the dead. However, over the last hundred years or so, some Churches have permitted cremation.

In Britain today, six out of ten funerals take place at a crematorium.

A relative of Indian spiritual leader Maharishi Mahesh Yogi offers prayers as he prepares to light the funeral pyre on the banks of India's Ganges River.

Ritual symbols

Colours

Colours associated with death and funerals are more to do with culture than religion. In the West, black is associated with death, and people may wear black to funerals. In the East, people tend to use white to represent death.

Monuments

Religions that prefer cremation to burial (where ashes are scattered) tend not to build memorials to the dead.

However, there is a tradition in Buddhism of placing the ashes of a great Buddhist teacher in a stupa. Originally, a **stupa** was a dome-shaped mound, but they have developed into elaborate buildings.

The stupa (below) developed into more elaborate buildings, like this **pagoda** (right).

The Taj Mahal was built by Shah Jahan, the Muslim Emperor of India in the seventeenth century, in memory of his third wife, Mumtaz Mahal. It is widely considered to be one of the most beautiful buildings in the world and stands as a symbol of eternal love.

Muslims are buried with no possessions, and graves are marked simply. Important royal or religious figures may have buildings dedicated to them, like the famous Taj Mahal in India.

Christian tombs can be quite elaborate in design. They may have inscriptions carved in marble or granite, such as a passage from the Bible, or a poem about the deceased. They may also have symbols of Christian beliefs about death, such as:
- a grieving angel – sorrow
- an arch or hands – meeting a deceased partner in heaven
- evergreen – eternal life
- ivy – faith
- a shell – resurrection
- a mermaid – Jesus: both God and human
- a cross, an anchor and a Bible – hardships in life, victory overcoming them, and reward in heaven
- a lamp – eternal life.

Mourning

It is important that close relatives and friends of the deceased have time to grieve and support each other.
- In Buddhism, ceremonies are held periodically after death. Mourners pray to pass on their own fortunate **karma** to the deceased to help them in their future life.
- In some Christian churches, men do not shave for 40 days. Special prayers are said for the deceased on particular days. Christians who visit the grave of a loved one place flowers on it.
- In Hinduism, mourning lasts for thirteen days. During that time, the deceased's family may not perform any religious acts, and may not cook. They rely on friends to provide food for them. Men do not shave for ten days after the death.
- In Judaism, there are four stages of mourning that last for eleven months. Each year after the death, relatives say a special prayer and light a candle. When Jews visit a grave, they leave a stone on it to show that the person has not been forgotten.

Stones are placed on Jewish graves when they have been visited.

- In Islam, a three-day period for mourning is observed for loved ones, but a widow must mourn for four months and ten days. Graves are not marked with flowers.
- In Sikhism, mourning lasts for ten days, during which there are readings from the Guru Granth Sahib and special prayers are said.

Knowledge check

1. How do Buddhists, Hindus and Sikhs believe a dead body should be disposed of?
2. How do Christians believe a dead body should be disposed of?
3. What is a stupa?
4. What does a shell represent on a Christian tomb?
5. How do Christians show respect for a dead person when they visit a grave?
6. How long does mourning last in Hinduism?
7. How do Jews show that they have visited a grave?

Activity A

In this country, when a person dies, sympathy cards are sent to the people who were closest to them.

1. Design a sympathy card using some of the symbols described in this chapter.
2. Inside, write a note to the bereaved person expressing sorrow for their loss. Imagine that they have a religious faith, and use your knowledge and understanding of that faith to write some comforting words.

Activity B

What do religious funerals tell you about religious beliefs about death? Look at things people do, words that are said and symbols that are used. How do they express what people believe?

Activity C

1. Write an account of a Hindu, Buddhist or Sikh funeral, and an account of either a Muslim or Jewish funeral.
2. Compare the two: what is similar and what is different? You might find some photographs to illustrate your accounts.

Activity D

'Funerals are for the living, not the dead.'

1. What do you think is meant by this? Do you agree with it? Try to find examples from religious death rites of how they support those who mourn.
2. Try also to find examples of how religious funerals are meant to help the departed in the afterlife.

The big assignment

Task
To design a catalogue of religious **artefacts** for schools.

Objectives
- To find out about artefacts that are used by religious people to help them to worship.
- To understand how artefacts are used in worship.
- To understand how artefacts aid worship.

Outcome
To produce a paper or electronic catalogue describing a range of religious artefacts and explaining their uses in worship.

You should include information about:

- the religious artefacts
- their usage
- symbolism
- their religious significance

Guidance

1. Work in groups of six. Each member of the group should specialise in a different religious tradition.
2. Each person in the group should research a range of artefacts from their specialist faith.
3. For each artefact, find out:
   - what it looks like
   - what it is made of
   - any symbolism associated with it
   - what it is used for
   - who uses it
   - how it is used
   - where it is used
   - how it is treated
   - what special conditions are associated with its use
   - why it is important.
4. Build up a collection of photographs of artefacts you have researched.
5. Put together your photographs and research outcomes as either:
   - hard-copy pages, or
   - electronic pages.
6. Assemble the pages from all group members to create a catalogue.

Assessment

You will be assessed on:
- ✓ how well you use specialist vocabulary
- ✓ your ability to describe how artefacts are used in worship
- ✓ how well you explain why artefacts are used in worship
- ✓ your ability to explain the importance of artefacts for worshippers.

2.1 Are religion and science in conflict?

Learning objectives

You will...
- learn about different views about science and religion
- understand why different people have different views about science and religion
- evaluate different views about science and religion and form your own opinion.

Different views

Religion and science are in conflict

Some people find religion difficult to accept because they think you cannot be religious and hold a scientific view of the world at the same time.

They say that religion and science are in conflict.

Science explains how the universe came about and how life evolved. Religious teachings don't explain anything very important. Most of them are just plain stupid.

Religious teachings about the origins of the universe and life came a long time before science. Although some religious people in this country believe that religious accounts of God creating the universe are literally true, most do not.
- They believe, for example, that the universe came about as a result of the Big Bang 13.5 billion years ago, but that God caused it to happen.
- They believe that life evolved (and is still evolving) as creatures adapt to their environments, but that the process is directed by God.

Religion and science are independent

Some people think that science and religion are about completely different things: science is about the physical world, and religion is about the spiritual world.

They say that religion and science are independent.

> It is possible to accept science and be religious at the same time.
> - Science is about what the universe is made of, and how it works.
> - Religion is about the meaning and purpose of life, and how humans should live in harmony with each other and their environment.

Science tries to answer questions like, 'How did the universe begin?' Religion tackles the problem of why the universe exists at all. So they are not in conflict.

Religion and science are in dialogue

Some people think that science and religion can help each other. Religious belief can inspire scientists to make greater discoveries; science stops religions from making false claims and teachings.

They say that religion and science are in dialogue.

> - Having a scientific understanding of the universe need not make a religious person's faith any weaker.
> - Having a religious faith does not make science any less important or less true.

Looking at the universe scientifically and religiously gives a complete picture of what it is about.

God created the world and human beings in it. It is part of God's plan for humans to find out about his creation through science.

33

What does Britain think?

A survey of more than 2000 British adults found that:
- 10 per cent of people believe religion and science to be in conflict.
- 75 per cent said that science can explain many things, but not everything.
- 47 per cent said that scientific understanding challenges religious beliefs, but it is possible to hold both views.
- 26 per cent said that science neither supports nor weakens religion.

Knowledge check

1. Give an example of why some people think religion and science are in conflict.
2. According to people who think that religion and science are independent of each other, what is the main difference between them?
3. According to people who think that religion and science are in dialogue, how can they work together?

Activity A

1. Look again at the information about people who believe that science and religion are independent. Make two lists of questions:
   a) those that are to do with science
   b) those that are to do with religion.
2. Find some pictures to illustrate each of them, and make a wall display of Religion and Science.

Activity B

1. Conduct a survey of pupils in your school to find out if they think:
   - religion and science are in conflict
   - religion and science are independent
   - religion and science are in dialogue.
2. How do your results compare to the survey mentioned above? Did you find similar or different results?
3. Use ICT to display the results of your survey.

Activity C

Imagine you are a television journalist. You are interviewing three people representing the three viewpoints on religion and science.

Write a transcript (record) of the discussion, emphasising any points of agreement as well as disagreement.

Activity D

1. What do you think about the relationship between science and religion?
   - Are they in conflict?
   - Are they independent of each other?
   - Are they in dialogue with each other?
2. Investigate these questions and then present your view.

2.2 Where did life come from?

Learning objectives

You will ...
- find out about different theories of the origins of life
- understand the reasons people give to support the theories
- understand religious views about the theories
- compare the different theories.

Which came first: the chicken or the egg?

Planet Earth is about 4.5 billion years old. For the first half billion years, it was bombarded by meteors and asteroids, so nothing could have lived. So, how did life arise? Where did it come from?

There are two main theories about the origins of life.

Biogenesis: The idea that life can only come from things that are already living.

Abiogenesis: The idea that life can be created from non-living stuff.

35

Nearly 2500 years ago, a philosopher called Aristotle said that living things could come about by *spontaneous generation*: they just appear. For example, when meat goes rotten, maggots appear. Aristotle said that the maggots came from the rotten meat: ABIOGENESIS.

In the seventeenth century, a scientist called Francesco Redi proved that rotten meat did not produce maggots; maggots come from flies: BIOGENESIS.

In the nineteenth century, Louis Pasteur showed that food doesn't go bad on its own. Micro-organisms like bacteria are in the air and they breed in food: BIOGENESIS.

In the 1950s two scientists, Stanley Miller and Harold Urey, mixed chemicals known to have been present on Earth 3.9 billion years ago. The Miller-Urey experiment attempted to recreate the conditions on Earth early in its history to see if life could have arisen from non-living chemicals. In a laboratory, they created electric storms in the chemicals. After a week, amino acids had formed. Amino acids are the building blocks of life: ABIOGENESIS.

Aristotle and Louis Pasteur.

So where did life come from?

For supporters of abiogenesis, the building blocks of life were created from chemicals in the oceans of the primitive world.

VS

For supporters of biogenesis, the building blocks of life on Earth must have come from somewhere else. Perhaps they fell to Earth on meteorites.

What's this got to do with religion?

Most religions teach that God created life. So they can believe one of three things:
- Abiogenesis. God made the world with the right conditions for life to come about. More complex organisms then evolved.
- Biogenesis. The building blocks of life were created by God. More complex organisms evolved from them.
- Creationism. God created living things as they are. The things created by God can't produce new forms: only God can.

And no shrub of the field had yet appeared on the earth and no plant of the field had yet sprung up, for the LORD God had not sent rain on the earth and there was no man to work the ground, but streams came up from the earth and watered the whole surface of the ground – the LORD God formed the man from the dust of the ground and breathed into his nostrils the breath of life, and the man became a living being.

(Genesis 2:5–7)

Have not those who disbelieve known that the heavens and the earth were of one piece, then we parted them, and we made every living thing of water? Will they not then believe?

(Qur'an, 21:21)

According to Buddhist teachings, the Buddha refused to answer questions about the origins of the universe and life. He said: 'I have not explained these things. Why have I not explained them? Because it is not useful; it is not fundamentally connected with the spiritual life.'

Knowledge check

1. What is biogenesis?
2. Who first suggested that life could come about by spontaneous generation?
3. What did Francesco Redi prove?
4. Who showed that amino acids can form from non-living chemicals?
5. What is creationism?

Activity A

Some people say that God must be responsible for the creation of life because of its beauty and complexity.

1. Find photographs of natural beauty in the environment. Try to say why you find them beautiful.
2. Do you think there must be a God to create such beauty? Give reasons for your answer.

Activity B

Find out about the teachings of one religion on the origins of life. Remember that not everyone with the same faith agrees, and you should explain why they disagree. You could present your findings in the form of a script for a television documentary programme.

Activity C

1. Read the quotations from the Bible and the Qur'an above. What do they have in common with each other?
2. What do they have in common with scientific theories about the Big Bang, abiogenesis and biogenesis?
3. Do the quotations show that religion and science are in conflict?

Activity D

1. Do you agree with the Buddha's view that religious people do not need to have a view on the origins of life? Give reasons for your answer.
2. Would all religious people agree with you?

2.3 What do religious people think about evolution?

> ### Learning objectives
> You will …
> - learn about what evolution means
> - understand what the theory of evolution is about
> - understand what theistic evolution means
> - understand why some religious people do not accept evolution
> - evaluate different views about evolution.

What is evolution?

Evolution is a process of changes in populations of plants and animals from generation to generation. The theory of evolution was put forward by Charles Darwin in the nineteenth century.

As changes take place over long periods of time, new species come into being.
- Most scientists believe that, billions of years ago, chemicals randomly organised themselves into a molecule that could make copies of itself.
- This was the origin of every living thing we see today (as well as those we no longer see, like dinosaurs).
- Through evolution, that simple life form has been shaped into every living species on Earth.
- So all living things can be traced back to a common ancestor.

The Charles Darwin statue outside the Museum and Library in Shrewsbury, Shropshire. The building is the original Shrewsbury School building where Darwin was a pupil.

An example of evolution at work

One of the most straightforward examples of evolution is that of the giraffe. Evolutionary theory attempts to explain why and how the giraffe developed long front legs and a long neck.

> Giraffes live in dry places where the only vegetation is at the tops of trees.

> Originally giraffes had short necks and were able to nibble at the lowest branches.

> When the lower leaves were eaten, the tallest animals with the longest necks were able to get to leaves higher up.

> The giraffes with the shortest necks died.

> The longer-necked giraffes survived and produced young who inherited their parents' longer necks.

> As the process was repeated over generations, only giraffes with the longest necks survived and reproduced.

The evolution of the giraffe.

By this process long-continued ... it seems to me almost certain that an ordinary hoofed quadruped might be converted into a giraffe.

(Charles Darwin, The Origin of Species)

Most religious people accept that evolution is the most likely explanation for the development of life on Earth. They would say:
- There is a God.
- God created the universe and all life within it.
- God directs the process of evolution within creation to develop and create new creatures.
- God used evolution to develop human life.

The idea that God directs evolution is called **theistic evolution**.

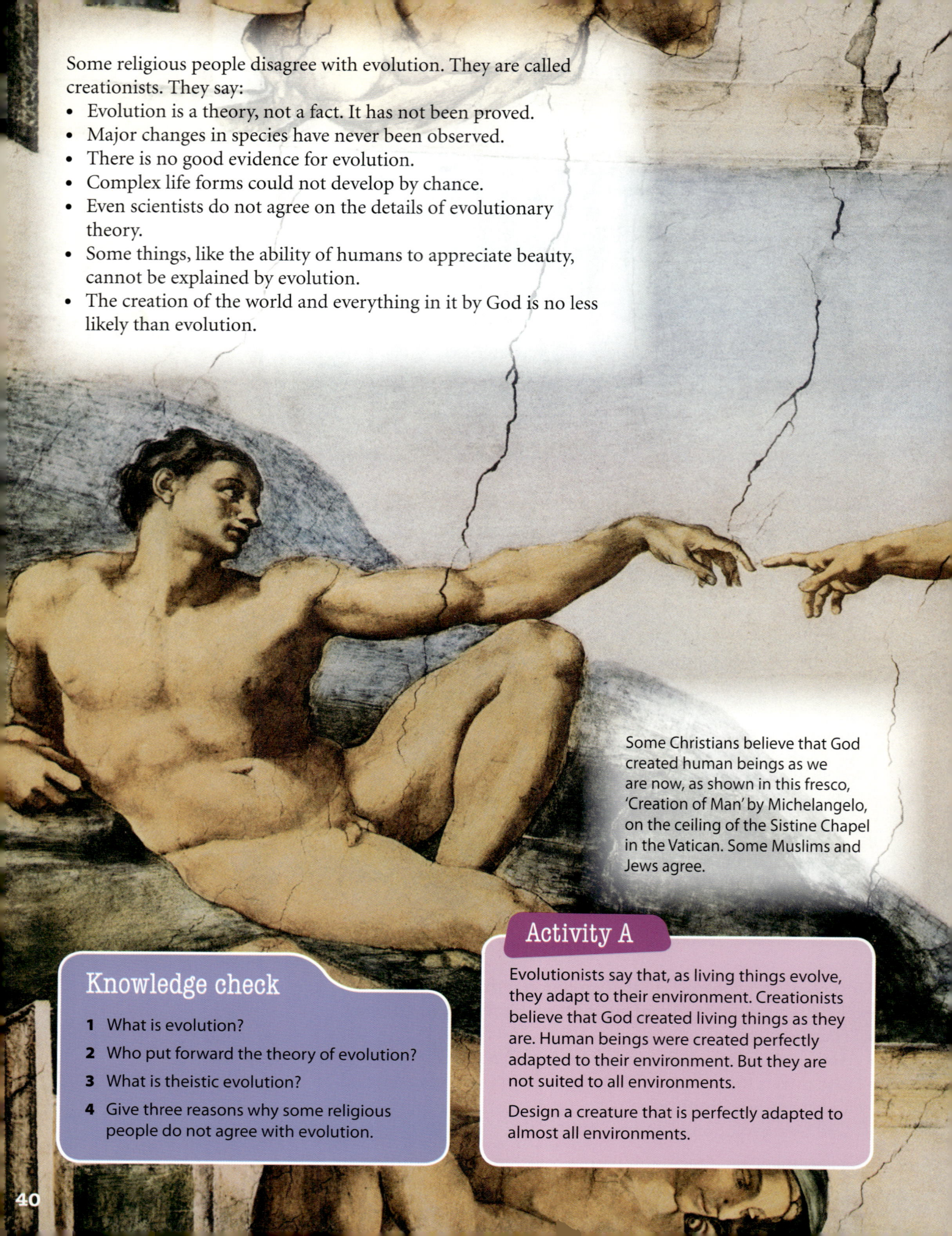

Some religious people disagree with evolution. They are called creationists. They say:
- Evolution is a theory, not a fact. It has not been proved.
- Major changes in species have never been observed.
- There is no good evidence for evolution.
- Complex life forms could not develop by chance.
- Even scientists do not agree on the details of evolutionary theory.
- Some things, like the ability of humans to appreciate beauty, cannot be explained by evolution.
- The creation of the world and everything in it by God is no less likely than evolution.

Some Christians believe that God created human beings as we are now, as shown in this fresco, 'Creation of Man' by Michelangelo, on the ceiling of the Sistine Chapel in the Vatican. Some Muslims and Jews agree.

Knowledge check

1. What is evolution?
2. Who put forward the theory of evolution?
3. What is theistic evolution?
4. Give three reasons why some religious people do not agree with evolution.

Activity A

Evolutionists say that, as living things evolve, they adapt to their environment. Creationists believe that God created living things as they are. Human beings were created perfectly adapted to their environment. But they are not suited to all environments.

Design a creature that is perfectly adapted to almost all environments.

Activity B

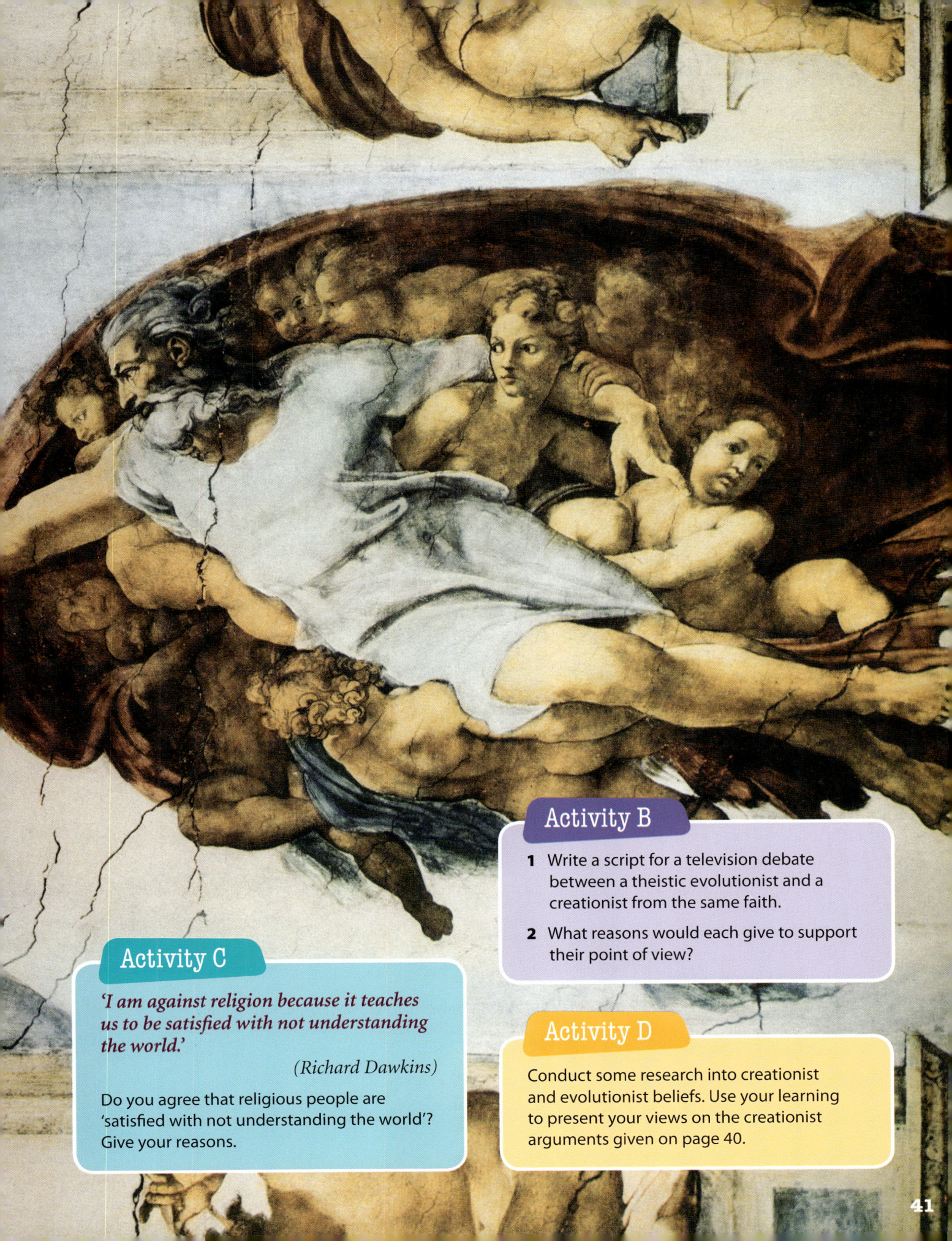

1 Write a script for a television debate between a theistic evolutionist and a creationist from the same faith.
2 What reasons would each give to support their point of view?

Activity C

'I am against religion because it teaches us to be satisfied with not understanding the world.'

(Richard Dawkins)

Do you agree that religious people are 'satisfied with not understanding the world'? Give your reasons.

Activity D

Conduct some research into creationist and evolutionist beliefs. Use your learning to present your views on the creationist arguments given on page 40.

2.4 Are humans special?

Learning objectives

You will...
- compare similarities and differences between human beings and other animals
- find out about unique features of human beings
- find out why religions teach that human beings are special.

Animals and humans

According to evolutionary science, all living things are descended from a common ancestor. If this is true, then it follows that:
- all living things are related to one another, and
- human beings are just one species of animal.

Our closest relatives are gorillas and chimpanzees. It is thought that we share 98.4 per cent of our genetic make-up with them.

How are we different?

We share many characteristics with other primates. These include:
- a well-developed brain
- five digits on each limb
- opposable thumbs
- fingernails and toenails
- usually one young per pregnancy
- the ability to stand on two feet.

What makes humans different is our brainpower. We have 300,000 times more brain cells than a fly, and more complex brain networks than any other creature. This sets us apart from other animals, including chimps.

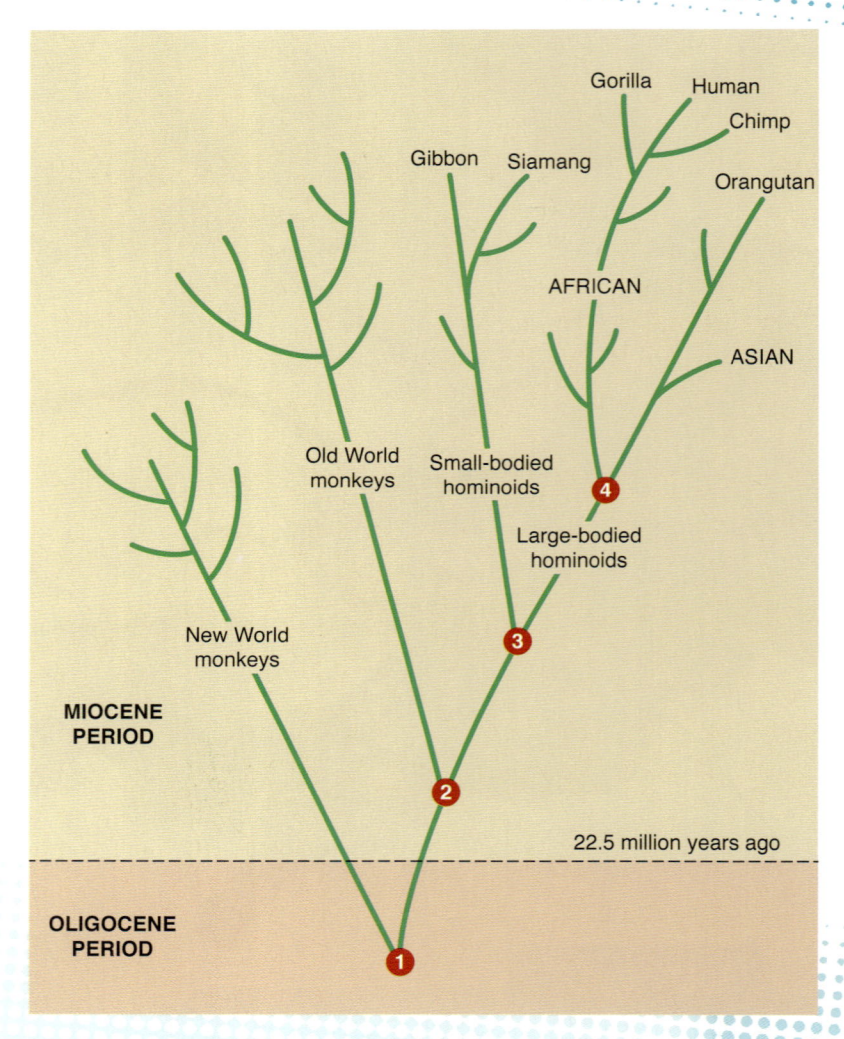

This diagram shows that humans come from the same ancestor (1) as other primates, but have developed differently.

Chimps patrol their territories and fight intruders.	Humans build sophisticated weapons to fight against competing nations.
Chimps can understand what other chimps are thinking.	Humans can understand what another person is thinking about a third person.
Chimps can make connections between their actions and rewards they may get for them afterwards.	Humans can make connections between what is happening now and what happened years ago, or what may happen in the future.
Chimps can feel for another chimp that is in pain.	Humans can feel for someone thousands of miles away, or even in a work of fiction.

What makes us special?

Many people might say that there are things about humans that set them so far apart from other animals that they are special. These things include:

- **a sense of morality** – our feelings of duty to protect our families may be a product of evolution. But humans also feel moral duties that go against evolution. For example, we think it is right to protect other animals, even if they are our natural predators or competitors for food.
- **a sense of spirituality** – the search for meaning and purpose in life, and thoughts about what may happen after we die, are unique to the human animal. We can also appreciate beauty and create beautiful things.

Religions teach that human beings are special.

The Abrahamic faiths (Judaism, Christianity and Islam) teach that all things were created by God. God created plant life and animals. He created humans separately, after everything else: they are his most important creation.

Hinduism teaches that living things experience many lifetimes, one after another, but they can free themselves from the cycle and become one with God (**moksha**). Human beings have senses of morality and spirituality, so they can do things that lead them to moksha.

Buddhism teaches that life is one thing that is shared by all things. All things can be born in any form, but it is incredibly rare to be born as a human being. Human beings can become enlightened, so they should use the opportunity to do so.

Sikhism teaches that a person has existed as any number of living things before becoming a human being. Only humans can make the moral and spiritual choices to stop being reborn and become one with God (**mukti**). But, in the end, it is up to God whether the cycle of birth and **rebirth** ends.

The Buddha explained that it was very rare to be born as a human being. He said to his followers:

> Imagine a man throwing into the ocean a piece of wood with a hole in it. It is carried to and fro across the waters.
>
> Imagine, too, a turtle that can only see through one eye. It lives at the bottom of the ocean, and comes to the surface just once every hundred years.
>
> What are the chances of this turtle putting his head through the hole in the piece of wood?
>
> The chances of the turtle putting his head through the hole in the piece of wood are greater than the chance of being born as a human being.'

(Majjhima Nikaya 129)

Missed again!

Knowledge check

1. Why might some people say that human beings are just a species of animal?
2. Which animals are human beings most closely related to?
3. What do human beings have that no other animal has?
4. Which religions teach that human beings can stop being reborn and become one with God?
5. Which religion teaches that the purpose of life is to become enlightened?

Activity A

1. Which characteristics do human beings have in common with other animals? Which are unique to humans (i.e. what can we do that other animals can't)?
2. Draw up your ideas as a mind map or a Venn diagram.

Activity B

1. Choose one religion and find out what it teaches about human beings and other animals.
2. Write a set of questions that you could ask to find out what the teachings have to say about how special human life is.

Activity C

Do you think that human beings are special in a way that separates them from other animals? Or are we just a sophisticated form of animal? Try to give examples and reasons to support your answer.

Activity D

What does the Buddhist quotation on page 44 say about the differences between human beings and animals in Buddhism?

2.5 Is there a purpose to life?

Learning objectives

You will …
- understand why some people believe that human life has a purpose
- find out about religious teachings on the purpose of life
- think about your view on the purpose of life.

'The Ascension scenes from the Life of Christ', seventeenth century. It shows Jesus ascending to heaven after his resurrection. Heaven is represented by the nucleus of an atom, bringing all things together.

One of the things that separates human beings from other animals is their sense of spirituality.
- Humans are able to feel that they are more than just flesh and blood.
- They feel somehow connected to the world around them.
- They can believe that there is a meaning and a purpose to life.

Many people think that life (especially human life) is so complex that it can't have happened by chance. There must be a point to it. People are so different from other animals that their lives must have a special purpose. We are here for a reason.

Abrahamic religions believe the aim of life is eternal happiness after death on a spiritual plane. This is sometimes called salvation.

Christianity
- For Christians, salvation means being freed from the effects of sin. The possibility of eternal life is then opened up. Jesus made eternal life possible by his resurrection.

For God so loved the world that he gave his one and only Son, that whoever believes in him shall not perish but have eternal life.

(John 3:16)

- Christians believe that salvation is achieved by following Jesus and his teachings on loving God and other human beings.

Judaism

- Judaism teaches that Jewish people can achieve salvation because they have a special relationship with God.

The world stands on three things: on torah, on worship, and on acts of loving kindness.

(Talmud)

- So Jews follow God's laws, worship him, and care for other people.

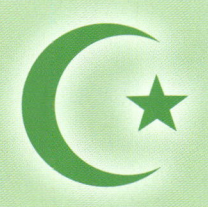

Islam

- Salvation is achieved through submission to the will of Allah.

The Apostle of Allah [said]: He who goes forth in the path of Allah … will go to Paradise.

(Hadith)

- Muslims follow Allah's path by practising the Five Pillars of Islam.

Eastern religions do not believe in salvation after death. They believe in rebirth after the death of the body.

Hinduism

- Hindus aim to achieve moksha. Moksha is an escape from lifetimes of existence to merge with God.

Aum: this imperishable word is the universe. It is explained as the past, the present, the future. Everything is the word Aum … Thus Aum is the soul. Whoever knows this enters by one's soul into the soul.

(Mandukya Upanishad)

- To achieve moksha, Hindus follow one or more of four paths (yogas): doing good to others; devoting oneself to the love of God; gaining a deep understanding of God; meditation.

Sikhism

- Sikhs believe that each person has a spark of God in them (a **soul**). The soul is taken back to join God when a person is finally released from the cycle of rebirth (mukti).

*A place in God's court can only be attained if we do service to others in this world … Wandering ascetics, warriors, celibates, holy men, none of them can obtain mukti without performing **sewa**.*

(Guru Granth Sahib)

- So Sikhism teaches that mukti is achieved only by serving people in one's community.

Buddhism

- For Buddhists, the aim of life is to attain **enlightenment**.

If a man can control his mind he can find the way to enlightenment, and all wisdom and virtue will naturally come to him.

(Buddha)

- Buddhists follow the Noble Eightfold Path to attain enlightenment.

The Buddha's enlightenment. Most Buddhists believe that everyone has the potential to be enlightened.

People who are not religious do not believe that human beings were put on Earth to fulfil a purpose. But this doesn't mean they believe life has no purpose.

Many non-religious people believe that each person should find a purpose in their own life – something to live for, to make the world a better place.

Knowledge check

1. Why do some people think that human life has a special purpose?
2. What does salvation mean?
3. Why do Christians believe salvation is possible?
4. What is mukti?
5. How do Hindus believe a person can achieve moksha?
6. How do Sikhs believe a person can achieve moksha?

A Buddhist writing tells the following story.

> A man went to the house of a close friend and, having become drunk on wine, lay down to sleep. The friend had to go out. Before he went, he took a priceless jewel and sewed it in the lining of the man's robe. The man was asleep and drunk and knew nothing about it.
>
> When the man got up, he set out on a long journey. He met great hardship as he couldn't afford food or clothing, and he had to make do as best he could.
>
> Later, the close friend happened to meet him. The friend said, 'Why are you having such a hard time? Some time ago, I wanted to make sure you could live comfortably, so I sewed a priceless jewel into the lining of your robe. It must still be there now. But you did not know about it, and really struggled to provide a living for yourself. How silly! Now you can use the jewel. Then you can have whatever you want and never experience poverty or hardship.'
>
> The story ends by saying: The Buddha is like this friend.
>
> (Lotus Sutra, Chapter 8)

Activity A

1 Find out about a religious person who devoted his or her life to a particular cause. What was their aim? How did they attempt to achieve it?

2 You could choose some key events in their life and draw them up on a storyboard.

Activity B

1 Investigate one religion's teachings about the purpose of life. Try to find some quotations from scripture relating to teachings about it.

2 How could they put the teachings into practice in their lives?

3 What is your view on the purpose of life?

Activity C

What does the Buddhist story on this page say about the meaning and purpose of life from a Buddhist point of view?

Activity D

1 Do any of the religious views on the purpose of life appeal to you? Why?

2 If none of them do, do you think that life has a purpose? If so, what is it? Is it the same for everybody? Give reasons for your answers.

2.6 What is death?

Learning objectives

You will...
- find out what religious people believe about life after death
- understand why people believe in life after death
- understand some symbols of death
- compare religious ideas about life after death.

Death – life's only certainty?

The American statesman and writer Benjamin Franklin once wrote: 'In this world nothing can be said to be certain, except death and taxes.'

The fact that every person's life will one day come to an end is one of the very few certainties about life. Yet we know very little about death. Even doctors and scientists do not all agree about the exact moment when death occurs.

Here are some more things that people have said about death.

Knowledge check

Read pages 50–51.

1. Why is it surprising that we know so little about death?
2. What do the quotations about death have in common?
3. What is a dualist?
4. What does death mean to religious people?

> Death ... the last sleep? No, the final awakening.

Walter Scott (Scottish writer)

> For death begins with life's first breath, and life begins at touch of death.

William Dunkerley (English writer)

> Nothing is dead; men feign themselves dead, and endure mock funerals ... and there they stand looking out of the window, sound and well, in some strange new disguise.

Ralph Waldo Emerson (American writer)

> When the body sinks into death, the essence of man is revealed.

Antoine de Saint-Exupery (French writer)

> Death is just another path, one that we all must take.

J. R. R. Tolkien (English writer)

> The day which we fear as our last is but the birthday of eternity.

Seneca (Roman statesman)

Is death the end?

Throughout history, many people have not been able to accept that the death of the human body is the end of life itself.

Religious people tend to be dualists. They believe that a human being is made up of a body and something else – a soul or mind. For them, death may be the end of the physical life of the body. But really it marks the separation of the body and the soul or mind. The body may stop working and disintegrate, but the soul or mind lives on unseen.

The nobles of ancient Egypt filled their tombs with statues of their servants, to work for them in the afterlife. These servants are providing food for their dead master.

Activity A

1 Find out about some of the symbols that people use to represent death. They could be religious or secular (non-religious).
2 You might try to design some of your own. Make a collage of the symbols.

Activity B

1 Investigate how some religious people have tried to show their beliefs and ideas about death through art.
2 You could present your findings as a PowerPoint® presentation or as a wall display.

Activity C

1 Conduct some research into the history of beliefs about death and the afterlife.
2 Draw out some of the similarities and differences between them, and show how religious views are influenced by culture.

Activity D

Why do people find it difficult to accept that life ends when the body dies?

You will need to conduct some research to answer this question, but you should also present your own thoughts and ideas. Refer to some religious teachings in your answer.

2.7 What is the soul?

Learning objectives

You will ...
- learn about what the soul means to different religious groups
- understand how thinking about the soul developed
- be able to interpret different understandings about the soul.

Different ideas about the soul

For many religious people, the soul is the essence of a person. This means it is the part of a person you cannot see, but that gives that person her or his individual identity.

But this hasn't always been its meaning.

- *Nephesh* is a Hebrew word that is used in the Jewish Biblical accounts of how God created life. It means 'a living being that has blood'. It is also translated as 'soul'. It is related to the word *naphash*, which means breath. The first human being became alive because God breathed into him.
So, in its original meaning, the soul was not separate from the body. It was a body that was alive. According to this view, when a body dies, the soul dies with it.
- After the death of Jesus, the Jews who became the first Christians started to believe that people could live on after death, because Jesus rose back to life after death. They thought that people's bodies would live again.
- Meanwhile, the ancient Greeks thought that the soul was an invisible part of a human being that lived on after death in a new body.
- Christians were influenced by Greek ideas, and started to think of the soul as being separate from the body. The soul decides how a person behaves. After death the soul leaves the body and is judged by God.

This picture is a nineteenth-century engraving showing the soul leaving the body at the moment of death.

- Hindus use the word **atman** for the soul. It literally means 'breath'. It is often translated as 'the self'. Hinduism teaches that the atman has always existed from the eternal past, and will exist into the eternal future.
  - All living things have atman: humans, animals and plants.
  - Atman can enter a body (birth) and leave a body (death). It gives life to the body, whether it is a human, animal or plant.
  - Atman moves from body to body until it realises its true nature. Its true nature is goodness and love; it is one with Brahman (God). In understanding this, it achieves moksha.
- Like Christians, Muslims believe that souls will be judged. Good souls will be rewarded with eternal life in heaven; bad souls will live forever in hell. This Hadith describes what souls look like in heaven:

'The inhabitants of Paradise are hairless, beardless and have black eyes, their youth does not pass away and their garments do not wear out.'

Knowledge check

1. What does the Hebrew word *nephesh* mean in English?
2. According to Judaism, where does life come from?
3. Who influenced Christian views about the soul?
4. What does atman mean?
5. What is the true nature of atman?

Activity A

1. The Qur'an describes heaven as a physical place where souls will live. Read Surah 76:11–22 and 47:15.
2. Draw and label a picture of what heaven may look like based on those descriptions. Then draw and label your own view of heaven.

Activity B

If it is true that good souls are rewarded after death in heaven, what changes would you make to your life to make sure of a place there?

Activity C

Find out more about Christian and Hindu views on the soul. Draw up a chart showing similarities and differences in their thinking. Try to find quotations to back up your conclusions.

Activity D

'People should enjoy life while they can, and not worry about what may, or may not, happen after they die.'

1. What is your view about this? Do you agree? Give reasons for your answer.
2. What reasons might someone have for having a different point of view from yours?

2.8 What is reincarnation?

> **Learning objectives**
> You will...
> - find out about samsara, karma and reincarnation
> - understand the differences between reincarnation and rebirth
> - be able to evaluate beliefs in karma and reincarnation.

Samsara

The Eastern religions – for example, Hinduism, Sikhism and Buddhism – teach that life does not begin at birth and end at death. Rather it flows from birth, through life, to death, and to rebirth. The word **samsara** means 'to flow', and is used to refer to the continuous flow or cycle of life.

Karma

Karma is the belief that good actions have good consequences, and bad actions have bad consequences. The word 'karma' means action. It is rather like a garden.
- Doing good deeds is like planting good seeds. Eventually they will grow to produce beautiful flowers.
- Doing bad deeds is like planting bad seeds. They will grow up to produce horrible weeds.
- But you usually don't know when the seeds will grow.
- Sometimes there are more flowers than weeds; at other times, there are more weeds than flowers.
- Be careful what you plant!

At any time, good things and bad things may happen to you. The law of karma says this is the result of the things you have done in the past. And when you die, there are still seeds that haven't yet grown. Your karma needs to be worked out in another lifetime.

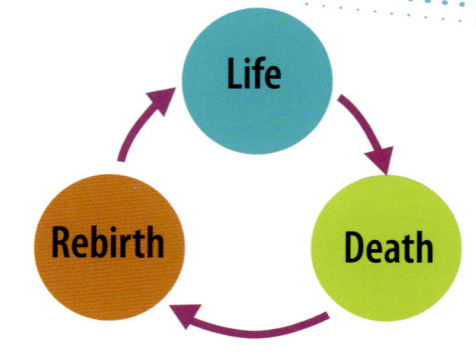

Samsara – the cycle of birth, death and rebirth.

> **Buddhism**
> *Just as a man's family welcomes him home after a long absence, so his own good deeds will welcome him when he moves from this world to the next.*
> (Dhammapada 220)

> **Hinduism**
> *Just as a man discards worn-out clothes and puts on new clothes, so the soul discards worn-out bodies and puts on new ones.*
> (Bhagavad Gita 2.2)

> **Sikhism**
> *Listen, listen to my advice, O my Mind! Only good deeds shall endure, and there may not be another chance.*
> (Guru Granth Sahib, 154)

Hindus and Sikhs believe that the soul comes from God, and is born into 8.4 million bodies as it journeys through samsara. As it journeys, it creates karma, both good and bad. Its aim is to get rid of the bad karma by only doing good deeds. Then it can be freed from samsara to merge back with God.

Until then, the soul is reborn into a new body each lifetime. This is called **reincarnation**.

Unlike Hindus and Sikhs, Buddhists do not believe in a God that created life, and they do not believe in a soul that makes something alive. They say that life just is. For them, it is a person's karma – the collection of good and bad deeds – that moves from lifetime to lifetime.

They call this rebirth rather than reincarnation.
- Reincarnation refers to a soul moving *into* a new body.
- Rebirth refers to karma being reborn *as* a new person.

Knowledge check

1. What does the word 'samsara' mean?
2. What does the word 'karma' mean?
3. According to the law of karma, why do bad things happen to people?
4. What is reincarnation?
5. Why don't Buddhists use the word 'reincarnation'?

Activity A

1. If you were able to choose, what would you want to be born (or reborn) as? Why? Give as many reasons as you can think of.
2. You could present your answer as a mind map.

Activity B

1. Write a script for a discussion between someone who believes in karma and someone who doesn't. Each is trying to persuade the other that they are right.
2. How would the person who believes in karma explain it? What examples would they give to persuade the other person? What examples may be put forward to deny the existence of karma?

Activity C

1. What sorts of evidence would be needed to show that human beings are reincarnated or reborn?
2. Conduct some research to find out what sorts of proof people offer to support their belief in reincarnation.

Activity D

'After all, it is not more surprising to be born twice than it is to be born once.'
Voltaire (eighteenth-century French writer)

1. What is your view of Voltaire's statement? What reasons might someone in the twenty-first century have for agreeing with him?
2. Do you believe in reincarnation? Give reasons for your answer.

The big assignment

Task
To write a report on the relationship between science and religion.

Objectives
- To find out about religious beliefs and teachings about scientific issues.
- To understand how conflict between science and religion can be resolved.
- To consider your own views about the issues.

Outcome

The Royal Society is an organisation whose members are leading scientists in Britain and abroad. They are concerned that religion and science seem to be in conflict.

Imagine that they have asked you to write a report on religious beliefs and teachings about scientific issues. Your report will consist of information about the teachings, and a letter to the Society outlining your views on whether science and religion are in conflict.

You should cover one or two of the following issues:

- Where did life come from?
- What do religious people think about evolution?
- Are humans different from other animals?
- What is death?
- Is there a purpose to life?
- What do religious people believe about life after death?

Guidance

1. Divide the class into six groups. Each group should specialise in a different religious tradition:
   - Buddhism
   - Christianity
   - Hinduism
   - Islam
   - Judaism
   - Sikhism.

2. Each person in the group should research one or two issues from the viewpoint of their group's specialist faith.

3. Present the results of the research on each issue in the form of an illustrated report.

4. For each issue, write a paragraph explaining whether it shows that religion and science are in conflict or not.

5. Put together the reports as either:
   - hard-copy pages, or
   - electronic pages.

6. Assemble the pages from all group members to create a group report.

7. Assemble the reports from all the groups to make the final report.

8. If your final report is electronic, you could post it on your school website.

Assessment

You will be assessed on:
- ✓ how well you use specialist vocabulary
- ✓ your ability to describe the issues
- ✓ your ability to explain religious views about the issues
- ✓ your ability to explain whether religion and science are in conflict.

3.1 Do humans have rights?

Learning objectives

You will ...
- learn what human rights are
- understand why and how rights and responsibilities are linked
- understand why some people disagree with the UDHR
- interpret religious views about human rights.

Rights and responsibilities

One of the things that separate human beings from other animals is that humans are able to decide which actions are right and which are wrong. People ought to do what is right and avoid what is wrong.

Because of this, people have a duty or responsibility to treat other people fairly.

And this means that people have a right to be treated fairly.

So there is a strong relationship between rights and responsibilities. Every rule about how to treat others could be rewritten as a statement of a right on how people should be treated.

For example:

- **Rule:** Do not kill another human being.
- **Right:** All human beings have the right to life.

It works the other way round, too. Every right has a corresponding duty or rule:

- **Right:** Everyone has the right to own property.
- **Rule:** Do not take other people's property.

Knowledge check

Look at pages 58–61.
1. Why do people have the right to be treated fairly?
2. What does UDHR stand for?
3. How did the UDHR originate?
4. How many articles are there in the UDHR?
5. What were the Four Freedoms?
6. Why have some Muslim countries disagreed with the UDHR?

All human beings are born free and equal in dignity and rights. They are endowed with reason and conscience and should act towards one another in a spirit of brotherhood.

What is the Universal Declaration of Human Rights?

Before and during the Second World War, the German government was responsible for some horrific cruelty to millions of people. The world was shocked. So, in 1948, the United Nations agreed to a set of 30 articles (statements) about the rights and freedoms that all people are entitled to. They are called the Universal Declaration of Human Rights (UDHR).

Here are some of them:

1 Everyone has the right to **life** and to live in **freedom** and **safety**.

2 Everyone has the right to be **free from harm**.

3 Everyone has the right to be **treated fairly by the law**.

4 Everyone should be considered **innocent** until **guilt is proved**.

5 **No one** has the right to **enter your home, read your messages** or **bother you** or your family without a good reason.

6 Everyone has the right to **marry and have a family**.

7 Everyone has the right to **own property** and possessions.

8 Everyone has the right to their own **beliefs** and to **choose** their **religion**.

9 Everyone has the right to **say what they think**.

10 Everyone has the right to help **choose the government** of their country.

11 Everyone has the right to **work** for a **fair wage** in **safety**.

12 Everyone has the right to **time off work**.

13 Everyone has the right to a **healthy lifestyle** and **medical help** if they are ill.

14 Everyone has the right to go to **school**.

15 Everyone must **respect the rights of others**.

16 **No one has the right to take away any of the rights of others**.

Eleanor Roosevelt, wife of President Franklin Roosevelt, holding a Universal Declaration of Human Rights poster, November 1949.

Does everyone agree with the Universal Declaration of Human Rights?

The second article of the UDHR says:

Everyone is entitled to all the rights and freedoms set forth in this Declaration, without distinction of any kind, such as race, colour, sex, language, religion, political or other opinion, national or social origin, property, birth or other status.

Support for human rights

- Jesus said,

'The Spirit of the Lord is on me, because he has anointed me to preach good news to the poor. He has sent me to proclaim freedom for the prisoners and recovery of sight for the blind, to release the oppressed …'

(Luke 4:18)

- The Dalai Lama is the spiritual leader of the Buddhist people of Tibet. He has won many awards for his work in the field of human rights. He says:

'All human beings, whatever their cultural or historical background, suffer when they are intimidated, imprisoned or tortured … We must, therefore, insist on a global agreement, not only on the need to respect human rights worldwide, but also on the definition of these rights … for it is the nature of all human beings to yearn for freedom, equality and dignity, and they have an equal right to achieve that.'

- Mahatma Gandhi was a Hindu leader in India when the British ruled there. Human rights leaders from around the world have named him as a source of inspiration in their struggles to achieve equal rights.

Arguments against human rights

- Some Muslim countries have said that parts of the UDHR go against some of their laws that are based on the teachings of the Qur'an (**Shari'ah**). For example, the UDHR says it applies to all people equally, but Shari'ah has some different laws for men and women.
- Some people think that the rights to believe whatever you want or say whatever you think can be dangerous.
- Some people think that religion itself can be dangerous. They say that the world would be a better place if there were freedom *from* religion rather than freedom *of* religion.

Activity A

1. Read the verse from the Bible, Luke 4:18 on page 60.
2. Some people think that this verse shows that Jesus cared about human rights. Which rights from the UDHR might Jesus' words match up with?
3. Use the Internet to find some examples of posters campaigning for human rights.
4. Design your own human rights poster to promote Jesus' statement.

Activity B

1. Choose five of the articles from the UDHR that you strongly agree with. Explain why you think they are particularly important.
2. You could find examples in the news of where these rights are being abused to illustrate your view.
3. Try to turn your top five rights into rules.

Activity C

1. Look up either the Ten Commandments or the Five Precepts and turn them into a list of rights.
2. Then write a speech or an article for a magazine to explain to people why human rights are important in Judaism, Christianity or Buddhism.

Activity D

'Everyone has the right to their own beliefs, to state their own opinions and to choose their own religion.'

1. Explain why some people would disagree with this.
2. Does the UDHR allow people to promote *any* belief or opinion, no matter what it is? What is your view, and why?

3.2 Are there religious rights?

Learning objectives

You will...
- learn about the laws that guarantee religious rights in Britain
- understand how the law may be applied in individual cases
- analyse and judge cases of alleged abuse of religious rights.

The European Convention on Human Rights

Inspired by the Universal Declaration of Human Rights, the countries of Europe drew up their own European Convention on Human Rights (ECHR) in 1950. Article 9 allows all Europeans:
- the right to freedom of belief and religion, and
- the right to practise a religion, so long as it doesn't break the law or go against other people's rights.

Key parts of the Convention were built into British law as the Human Rights Act in 2000.

How do human rights laws apply to religion in Britain?

Read the following case studies. They are all real, and all of them, except one, went to law. If you were judging them, what would your verdicts be?

Case 1

Shabina was a Muslim girl who attended a school in Luton, Bedfordshire. The school uniform allowed girls to wear **shalwar kameez** (baggy trousers and long, loose top) and **hijab** (headscarf) if they wished to dress modestly for religious reasons.

When she was 15, Shabina told her school that she wished to wear a **jilbab** (long, loose coat). The school would not allow it, because it was not school uniform.

Shabina claimed that the school was denying her the right to practise her religion.

Case 2

Sarika was a Sikh, aged 14, in a secondary school in South Wales. She wore a **kara**, a bangle that is one of the **Five Ks** – symbols of faith worn by Sikhs as a religious duty.

Sarika's school did not allow its pupils to wear jewellery, apart from a watch and a pair of ear studs. Sarika pointed out that her kara was not jewellery, but a religious symbol. The school threatened her with exclusion.

Case 3

Nadia worked for an airline company at a check-in desk. She was a Christian, and liked to wear a small cross on a chain around her neck outside her uniform. Her employers forbade the wearing of jewellery outside clothes and told her to remove it. She was suspended from duty. Nadia argued that the cross is a religious symbol in the same way a hijab is. Employees were allowed to wear the hijab.

Case 4

Aishah was a classroom assistant at a Christian faith school in West Yorkshire. She was a Muslim, and wore a **niqab** (a cloth covering the whole face except the eyes). When she was observed in the classroom, it was felt that the children could not hear her properly and could not see her facial expressions. She was asked to teach without the niqab, though she was told a hijab was perfectly acceptable. Aishah agreed not to wear the niqab, but only when no men were present. Her employers did not accept this and suspended her.

Case 5
At a Muslim faith school in Leicester, 90 per cent of the pupils were Muslims; the school was required by law to offer 10 per cent of its places to non-Muslims. The school uniform required girls to wear the hijab – including the non-Muslim girls. The school claimed it was just part of the uniform, like a shirt and tie.

Case 6
Lydia, aged 16, attended a school in West Sussex. She was a Christian, and was concerned about the number of young people having sexual relationships. Christianity disagrees with sex before marriage, so Lydia wore a ring – a 'purity ring' – as a symbol of her belief. In doing this she broke a school rule that forbade the wearing of jewellery. Lydia said it was not jewellery, but a religious symbol. The school threatened to exclude her if she continued to wear it.

So, what happened in each of the cases?

Case 1
Shabina initially lost her case at the high court, then won on appeal. The judge said the school did not have a good enough reason to deny her her rights. This ruling was overturned in the House of Lords. The Lords said that the school had gone to great lengths to accommodate Muslim beliefs about dress.

Case 2
Sarika won her case. The kara is a symbol of faith that Sikhs have a religious duty to wear.

Case 3
Nadia's employers changed their uniform policy to allow the wearing of jewellery. But a court would not make them pay for the wages she lost while she was suspended. It said that she didn't have a good reason to break the airline's uniform code because Christians don't have a religious duty to wear a cross.

Case 4
Aishah lost her case. She had not been discriminated against for religious reasons, but for educational ones.

Case 5
The school has not been challenged.

Case 6
Lydia lost her case. The judge said that wearing the ring was a personal choice, not a religious duty.

Knowledge check
1. When was the European Convention on Human Rights drawn up?
2. What two religious rights does article 9 of the ECHR guarantee?
3. When did the ECHR become law in Britain?

Activity A
1. Read through the case stories.
2. For each one, say what judgement you would have made had you been trying the case. Remember to give reasons.

Activity B
1. Choose one of the case stories. Imagine you are a television or newspaper reporter conducting an interview with people representing both sides of the argument.
2. Write a script of the interview in which both parties explain their views about the case.

Activity C
1. Read the verdicts (judgements; what happened in the cases).
2. For each one, say whether you agree or disagree, and give reasons for your views.

Activity D
In France, it is against the law to wear religious symbols in school.
1. Do you think it should be against the law in this country? Give reasons for your answer, using some of these case stories as examples.
2. Might religious people have different views from non-religious people? Explain your answer.

3.3 Why are people punished?

Learning objectives

You will ...
- find out about the purposes of punishment
- understand some religious viewpoints on the purposes of punishment
- present your views about punishment and back them up with reasons.

Did you know ...?
- In 1992, there were 44,000 people in prison in England and Wales.
- In 2011, there were 85,000 people in prison in England and Wales.
- It is thought that there will be more than 106,000 people in prison in 2013.
- It costs £47,000 a year to keep someone in prison – almost twice the average yearly salary for a worker in the UK.
- 95 per cent of prisoners are male.
- Government prison inspectors report that there is too little for prisoners to do, including education and employment.
- 60 per cent of people released from prison are reconvicted within a year.
- People who do community service are 7 per cent less likely to reoffend than those who receive prison sentences.
- 7 per cent of children have experience of their fathers being in prison.
- Just 36 per cent of people leaving prison go into education, training or employment.

Judges choose from a range of punishments according to the crime that has been committed. The ones shown here are: the death penalty, prison, a fine, community service.

What is the purpose of punishment?

If someone does something that is against the law and against the rights of others, they may be punished for it. Obviously, you cannot let people get away with it, otherwise there would be no point in having laws. But what is punishment for? What should it achieve?

There are four purposes of punishment.

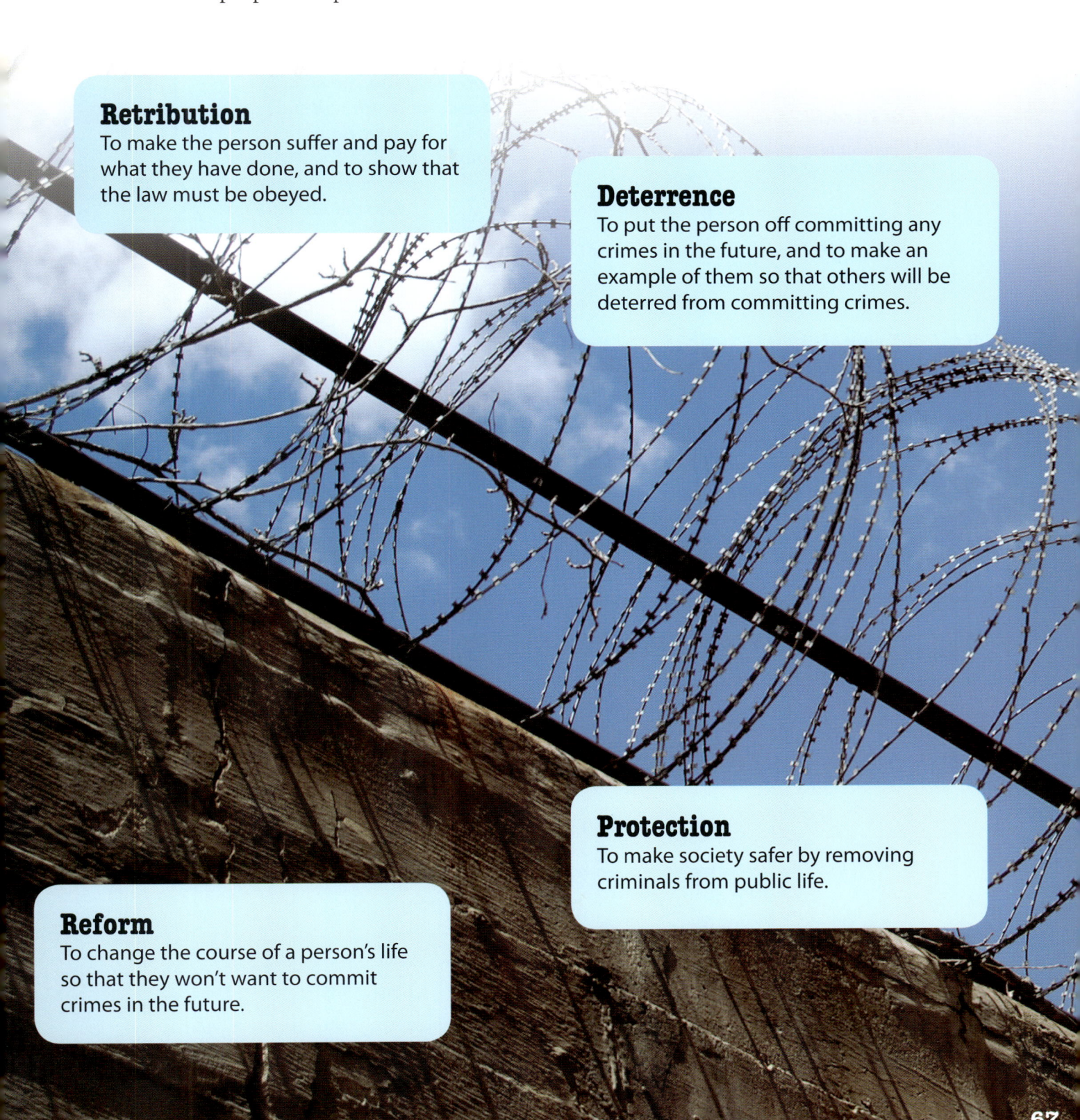

Retribution
To make the person suffer and pay for what they have done, and to show that the law must be obeyed.

Deterrence
To put the person off committing any crimes in the future, and to make an example of them so that others will be deterred from committing crimes.

Protection
To make society safer by removing criminals from public life.

Reform
To change the course of a person's life so that they won't want to commit crimes in the future.

Do religions agree with punishing people?

Religions agree that society cannot ignore people's wrongdoing.
But they disagree about:
- how people should be punished and
- the purposes of punishment.

A

If robbers be spared, all distinction between virtue and vice will disappear.
(from the Santiparva – Hinduism)

B

The rest of the people will hear of this and be afraid, and never again will such an evil thing be done among you.
(from the Jewish and Christian Bibles)

C

If the suffering of many disappears because of the suffering of one, that suffering would be something that someone with loving compassion would bring on, for the sake of himself and others.
(from the Bodhicaryavatara – Buddhism)

D

If one repents after committing this crime, and reforms, God redeems him. God is the Forgiver, the Most Merciful.
(Qur'an 5:39)

E

When someone is harming the public, farsighted people do not hurt him back, even if they are able.
(from the Bodhicaryavatara – Buddhism)

F

Do not seek revenge or bear a grudge against one of your people, but love your neighbour as yourself.
(from the Jewish and Christian Bibles)

G

There is rejoicing in the presence of the angels of God over one sinner who repents.
(Christian Bible)

H
And there is life for you in retaliation, O men of understanding, that you may ward off evil.
(Qur'an 2:179)

I
Strong intention is developed from a fear of suffering.
(from the Bodhicaryavatara – Buddhism)

Knowledge check

1. How much does it cost to keep a person in prison for a year?
2. What does retribution mean?
3. Which word means 'putting someone off committing further crimes'?
4. How can punishment make society safer?
5. What do the religions disagree about when it comes to punishment?

Activity A

1. Most forms of punishment have more than one purpose. Make a chart of the forms of punishment that are used in your school and home and the purposes of each of them.
2. Then say whether they are effective or not, in your opinion.

Activity B

1. Each of the quotations from religious texts relates to one or more of the four purposes of punishment. Write out the quotations in your own words and show which of the purposes they link with.
2. Then write a paragraph to say which of the quotations you particularly agree with, and why.

Activity C

1. Conduct some research into different views on punishment within the same religion.
2. Try to find some quotations from holy books or religious leaders to illustrate your account.
3. You could present your findings as a PowerPoint® presentation or a poster.
4. Which of the range of views is closest to your own?

Activity D

1. Find out about religious views on prison as a form of punishment.
2. How might the statistics in the 'did you know' panel on page 66 back up some points of view?
3. What is your view of prison as a form of punishment?

3.4 What is capital punishment?

Learning objectives

You will ...
- find out some facts about capital punishment
- understand why some people agree with capital punishment and some people oppose it
- analyse and compare religious views about capital punishment.

Capital punishment is a sentence of death as a penalty for committing a crime. It is sometimes called the **death penalty**.

Some facts about the death penalty
- Capital punishment is practised in 58 countries of the world.
- 96 countries have abolished the death penalty.
- More than 60 per cent of the world's population live in countries where executions take place.
- Common methods of execution include lethal injection, hanging, beheading, electrocution, stoning and shooting.
- Around 13,000 people have been executed in the USA since it gained independence in 1776.
- Today, around the world, 18,000 people are waiting for their death sentence to be carried out.
- Capital punishment was effectively abolished in Great Britain in 1965.
- The last execution in the UK took place in 1964.

The UK population is fairly evenly divided on the question of the death penalty.

Knowledge check

Read pages 70–71.

1. How many countries in the world practise the death penalty?
2. How many people around the world are waiting for the death penalty to be carried out?
3. When was capital punishment abolished in Great Britain?
4. Why might religions be against capital punishment?

People have different views about whether the death penalty should ever be used. Here are some of them.

Gassing used to be a method of execution. This gas chamber is in a former prison in Wyoming, USA.

> If someone murders someone else, then they should be killed.

> Ordinary people should be protected from murderers and rapists.

> Prison is not a harsh enough punishment for rapists and murderers.

> People might not commit violent crime if they know that they'll be killed for it.

> Killers are sick people. They need treatment to make them better, not punishment by death.

> What if you execute the wrong person? You can't bring them back to life.

> Why should the family of a murderer have to suffer? They've done nothing wrong.

> If murder is wrong, it should not be punished with another murder. Two wrongs don't make a right.

What do religions teach about capital punishment?

All religions teach that human life is special or sacred. This is one of the reasons that the right to life is protected in the Universal Declaration of Human Rights.

Yet within religions, people do not agree with each other about death as a punishment.

Buddhism teaches that all life should be protected and no harm should be done to it.

Yet some countries that have majority Buddhist populations have the death penalty.

Christianity teaches that human life is created by God and can only be taken by God.

Yet some Christian politicians are in favour of capital punishment.

Hinduism teaches ahimsa: the idea that violence should never be used.

Yet some Hindu scriptures call for the death penalty for some crimes.

The Jewish Bible teaches that death is an appropriate punishment for murder.

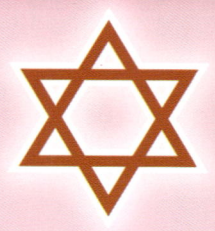

Yet Jewish scholars teach that capital punishment should be used only in very rare cases.

The Qur'an teaches that capital punishment is appropriate in certain cases. In some countries that practise Shari'ah law, death penalties are passed and carried out.

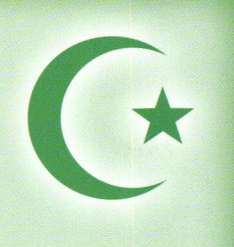

Yet the Qur'an also teaches that execution should be a last resort.

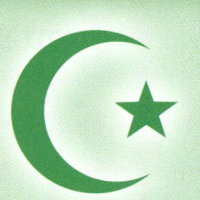

Activity A

Read the statements in the speech bubbles on page 71. Some support the idea of capital punishment and say it is a good thing; some are against it.

Make a display that clearly shows which statements support which point of view.

Activity B

Read the statements in the speech bubbles on page 71. Some support the idea of capital punishment and say it is a good thing; some are against it.

1. Sort them into two columns so it can be seen which statements support which point of view.
2. Try to add more statements to each side, including religious ones.
3. Then write a paragraph giving your own view of the death penalty and reasons for it.

Activity C

Make an information pack on religious and non-religious views about capital punishment. Include religious teachings and beliefs, public views on the death penalty from opinion polls, and your own view.

Activity D

1. Find out about the laws about capital punishment in Sri Lanka, Southern USA or Saudi Arabia.
2. Compare Sri Lankan laws with Buddhist teachings, Southern USA with Christian teachings, and Saudi Arabia with Muslim teachings.
3. Make a leaflet containing your findings. Include a section in which you give your view on your chosen area's laws on capital punishment.

3.5 How can people defend their rights?

Learning objectives

You will …
- find out about ways in which some religious people have defended their rights
- understand religious viewpoints on the use of violence in the defence of human rights
- evaluate views on the use of violence by religious people.

When the rights of individuals or communities are threatened, some people take action to protect their freedom. Religions have played their part in fighting for their rights and those of other people. Indeed, many people have seen it as their religious duty to do so.

Buddhism

- Thich Quang Duc was a Vietnamese Buddhist monk. On 11 June 1963, surrounded by his fellow monks, he set fire to himself and burned to death. He was drawing attention to the persecution of Buddhists by the government. They were denied religious freedom.

- Aung San Suu Kyi is a Buddhist from Burma. She spent fifteen years under house arrest for trying to form a government supported by the people. She was finally released in 2010.

Aung San Suu Kyi

Christianity

- Martin Luther King was a Christian minister who worked for racial equality in America in the 1950s and 1960s. He used non-violent methods for black people's rights to be recognised. He organised marches and demonstrations; made passionate speeches in churches, meeting halls and on television; he broke laws that were unfair to black people and was imprisoned several times. He was shot dead on 4 April 1968.

- Oscar Romero was an archbishop in El Salvador in Latin America. He spoke out against the government that denied religious rights, and he defended the rights of the poor. He was shot dead while he was conducting a religious service in a hospital chapel on 24 March 1980.

Martin Luther King.

Oscar Romero.

Hinduism

- Mahatma Gandhi was an Indian who lived when the British ruled in his country. He used non-violent means to protest against British rule and worked for Indian independence. He led marches, was imprisoned many times, and went on hunger strikes to force change. He was assassinated on 30 January 1948.

Gandhi spinning cotton to assert independence, 1925.

Islam

- The early months of 2011 have become known as the Arab Spring. People from countries with largely Muslim populations protested against government corruption, poverty, unemployment and human rights violations. They campaigned using strikes, demonstrations, marches and rallies. They spread their messages using social media like Facebook and Twitter.

During the Arab Spring, Muslims and Christians in Egypt guarded each other when they prayed. This photograph shows Christians joining hands to protect praying Muslims.

Judaism

- In 1939, Nazi Germany invaded Poland and began persecuting the Jews there. Mordechai Anielewicz was a young Jewish man who tried to persuade his fellow Jews to fight back. He became leader of the Jewish Combat Organisation and began armed resistance against the Nazis in Warsaw, to prevent Jews being taken to extermination camps. He died during the struggle on 8 May 1943.

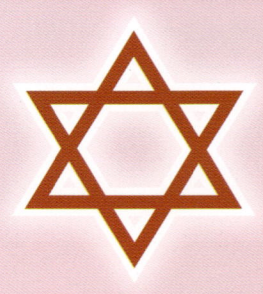

Sikhism

- Throughout their history, Sikhs have defended themselves against violations of their human rights and those of others, including the right to practise religion freely. The Ninth Guru, Tegh Bahadur, gave up his life on 11 November 1675 so that the Hindu community could continue to practise their faith. His two grandsons were also executed for refusing to give up Sikhism.

Knowledge check

1. How did Thich Quang Duc draw attention to the persecution of Buddhists in Vietnam?
2. What human right did Martin Luther King work for?
3. Against which government did Oscar Romero protest?
4. Which organisation did Mordechai Anielewicz lead?
5. For whose rights did Guru Tegh Bahadur give up his life?

Activity A

1. Find out more about four or five of the human rights campaigners featured in this chapter.
2. For each of them, design a T-shirt that could have been used as part of the campaign. You should think of a slogan and a symbol that would attract attention.

Activity B

1. Choose one of the human rights accounts featured in this chapter. Conduct some research into it, and produce an information leaflet.
2. Your leaflet should contain a short biography of the campaigner, or history of the campaign.
3. You should also include a section on the religious ideas and beliefs that motivated the actions.

Activity C

Make a list of the various ways that religious people could put their beliefs into practice when human rights are being threatened. Use the accounts featured in this chapter and others you find on the Internet to produce examples and illustrations for each. You could present your work as a poster or a booklet.

Activity D

'Religious people should never use violence, even when violence is used against them.'

1. What do you think about this statement?
2. Mahatma Gandhi, Martin Luther King and Aung San Suu Kyi all encouraged non-violent means of protest. Yet Mordechai Anielewicz led an armed revolt against the Nazis and the Sikh Gurus were prepared to fight to defend their rights. Write an account about the use of violence by religious people, using these and other examples. You should include information about religious teachings on the use of violence.
3. Finally, draw your own conclusion about the use of violence by religious people.

3.6 Do animals have rights?

Learning objectives

You will ...
- find out what the major religions teach about the relationship between human beings and animals
- understand how people interpret the teachings differently
- think about how animals should be treated in the light of religious teachings
- evaluate religious ideas about the treatment of animals.

Should animals have rights?

Animals do not have a sense of right and wrong. They will take from other animals, and even kill and eat them. No one would suggest that their actions are wrong or that they are evil. But human beings are moral creatures: we know what is right and what is wrong. This leads many people to believe that we ought to behave in a moral way towards other animals, even if they do not behave morally towards each other. This means that animals have rights.

However, animals cannot have the same rights as humans.

- The Universal Declaration of Human Rights says humans have the right to marry and freedom of religion. No one suggests that animals have these rights.
- But the UDHR also says that no one should be tortured or treated cruelly. Most people think that this applies to animals as well.
- The UDHR says that humans have a right to life. Most humans do not think that this applies to animals.

Religious views on animal rights

The Jewish, Christian and Muslim holy books agree that animals were created for the use of human beings.

> Then God said, 'Let us make mankind in our image, in our likeness, so that they may rule over the fish in the sea and the birds in the sky, over the livestock and all the wild animals, and over all the creatures that move along the ground.'
>
> *Bible (Judaism and Christianity)*

> It is God who provided for you all manner of livestock, that you may ride on some of them and from some you may get your food, and have other uses for them to satisfy your hearts' desires. It is on them, as on ships, that you make your journeys.
>
> *Qur'an 40:79–80*

Not everyone interprets these passages in the same way.

It should not be believed that all beings exist for the sake of the existence of man. On the contrary, all the other beings too have been intended for their own sakes and not for the sake of anything else.
Rabbi Moses ben Maimon (Judaism)

If you have men who will exclude any of God's creatures from the shelter of compassion and pity, you will have men who will deal likewise with their fellow men.
St Francis of Assisi (Christianity)

A good deed done to an animal is as praiseworthy as a good deed done to a human being, while an act of cruelty to an animal is as bad as an act of cruelty to a human being.
Prophet Muhammad (Islam)

Humans use animals for their own benefit. Do they ignore animal rights?

79

Hindu, Buddhist and Sikh holy books all teach that all life is equally precious: human, animal and plant.

If a person does not harm any living being ... and does not kill or cause others to kill, that person is a true spiritual practitioner.
Dhammapada (Buddhism)

He alone sees truly who sees the Lord the same in every creature ... seeing the same Lord everywhere, he does not harm himself or others.
Bhagavad Gita (Hinduism)

O Nanak, the True One is the Giver of all; He is revealed through His All-powerful Creative Nature.
Guru Granth Sahib (Sikhism)

Not everyone interprets these passages in the same way.

But Vinaya [book of rules for Buddhists] clearly mentions that meat which was purposely killed for you was not to be eaten, but in general was not prohibited ... I think practically in [the] northern part of Tibet, [there are] no vegetables. Very difficult. So that's [the] practical reason [to eat meat].
Dalai Lama (Buddhism)

Panchabali (sacrifice of five animals) is undertaken to get power, to get what you wish for and to ensure the well-being of the family. This puja (ceremony) will bring good consequences to the world and to Nepal.
Mod Raj Bhattarai (Hinduism)

When I became a Spiritual Sovereign ... I hunted various game in the forest, including bears, nilgaus and elks. Then, I left my home and ... I killed many ferocious lions and also nilgaus and elks.
Guru Gobind Singh (Sikhism)

Knowledge check

1. What do the Jewish, Christian and Muslim holy books teach about the relationship between humans and animals?
2. What does St Francis of Assisi say about people who are not compassionate towards animals?
3. What do the Hindu, Buddhist and Sikh holy books teach about the relationship between humans and animals?
4. Why is the Dalai Lama not a vegetarian?

Activity A

1. Draw a table or chart to show how human beings use animals for their benefit. (Use some of the ideas from this chapter and some of your own ideas.)
2. Which of these do you approve of, and which do you disagree with? Add your thoughts and reasons to your chart.

Activity B

Draw a mind map or spider diagram to show the different attitudes of the major religions to animals. Use information from this chapter and your own research.

Activity C

1. Animals are often used by human beings for medical research. Find out about religious and non-religious views about animal experimentation.
2. Present them on a poster, clearly showing arguments for and against animal testing for medical purposes. Add your own thoughts and feelings.

Activity D

1. What rights do you think animals have?
2. Compare your ideas with those of different religions. You could find out about Jainism and its attitude to and treatment of animals to include in your comparisons and evaluations.

3.7 Are we responsible for planet Earth?

> **Learning objectives**
> You will …
> - find out about the work of the Alliance of Religions and Conservation (ARC)
> - understand how ARC co-ordinates environmental projects run by religious organisations
> - link the environmental work of religious organisations with their core teachings.

What is ARC?

If your religion tells you … that the Creation of the world was an act of God, then it follows naturally … you ought to look after His Creation. It may not be sacred itself, but the One who created it is sacred – so it seems logical that humans ought to have a certain responsibility for it.
(HRH Prince Philip, founder of ARC)

The Alliance of Religions and Conservation (ARC) was founded in 1995 by Prince Philip. It is a charity that helps the major religions of the world to develop their own environmental programmes, based on their own core teachings, beliefs and practices. ARC currently works with eleven different faiths that together:

- represent the beliefs of 85 per cent of the population of the world – about five billion people
- manage 70 per cent of all tourist sites around the world
- own 7 per cent of the habitable land surface of the planet
- own and manage millions of buildings, community facilities, welfare networks, youth clubs, employment projects, and so on.

Prince Philip and the United Nations' Secretary-General Ban Ki-moon at ARC's Windsor Celebration in 2009.

What does ARC do?

Here are a few of the projects that ARC co-ordinates:

Green Pilgrimage Cities

Every year, millions of religious people go on **pilgrimages** – journeys to sites of religious importance. The Green Pilgrimage Network encourages pilgrims to respect the environment both on their journey and during their stay.

Pilgrimage sites and cities agree to provide facilities that safeguard the environment.

Amritsar (Sikhism) and Assisi (Christianity) are two of the first Green Pilgrimage Cities.

Faith in Food

Faith in Food is about people of faith eating food according to the values they promote.

Food goes to the heart of our relationship with the rest of creation. Our choices of what, when and how we eat have a huge impact upon the Earth, our fellow human beings and other living creatures.

(ARC)

Religious communities use food in worship and celebration, and many own or run schools, hospitals, restaurants and conference centres. Faith in Food works with them to ensure that the food they buy, grow or serve is consistent with their beliefs about caring for creation, and is kind to the Earth.

Living Churchyards

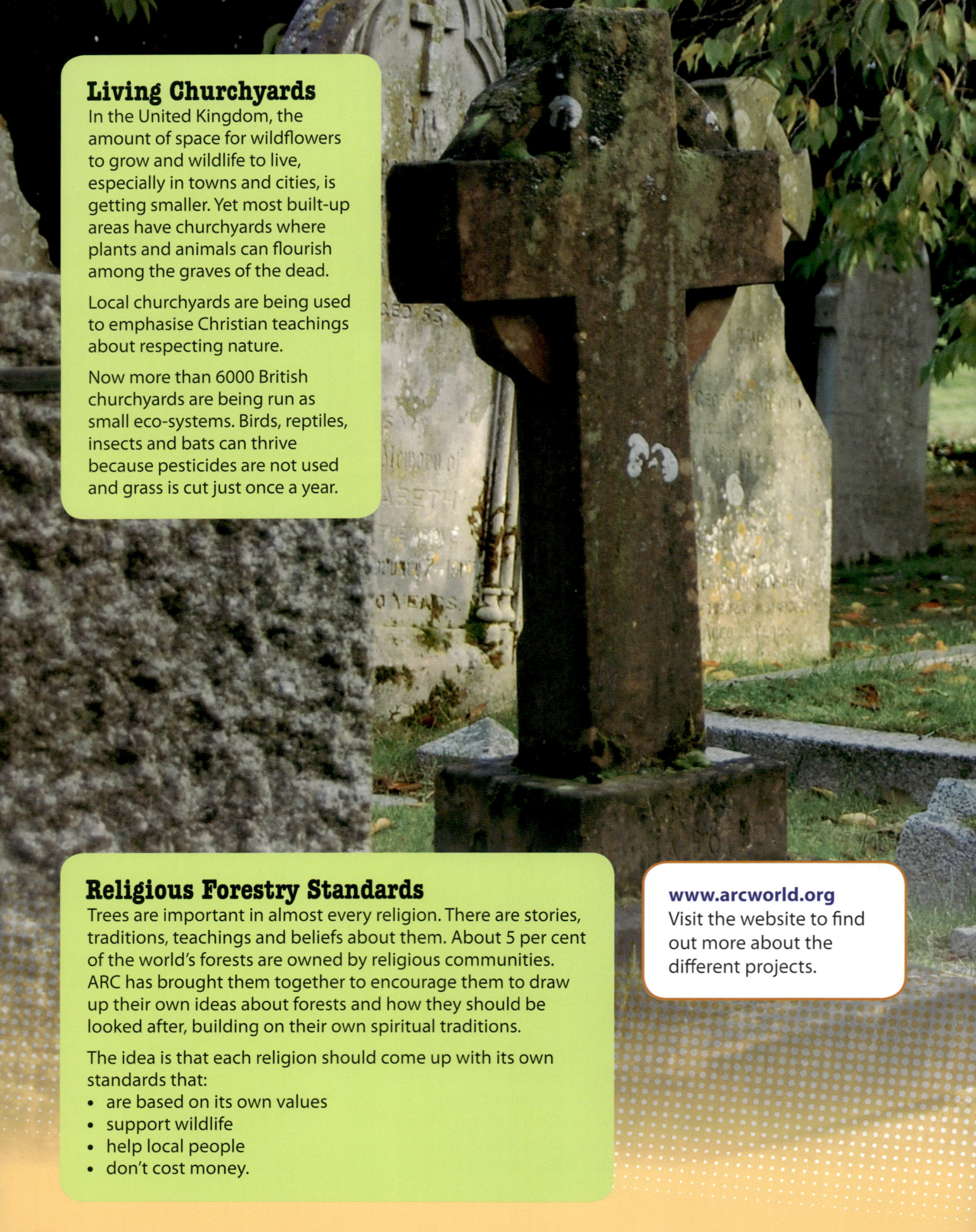

In the United Kingdom, the amount of space for wildflowers to grow and wildlife to live, especially in towns and cities, is getting smaller. Yet most built-up areas have churchyards where plants and animals can flourish among the graves of the dead.

Local churchyards are being used to emphasise Christian teachings about respecting nature.

Now more than 6000 British churchyards are being run as small eco-systems. Birds, reptiles, insects and bats can thrive because pesticides are not used and grass is cut just once a year.

Religious Forestry Standards

Trees are important in almost every religion. There are stories, traditions, teachings and beliefs about them. About 5 per cent of the world's forests are owned by religious communities. ARC has brought them together to encourage them to draw up their own ideas about forests and how they should be looked after, building on their own spiritual traditions.

The idea is that each religion should come up with its own standards that:
- are based on its own values
- support wildlife
- help local people
- don't cost money.

www.arcworld.org
Visit the website to find out more about the different projects.

Knowledge check

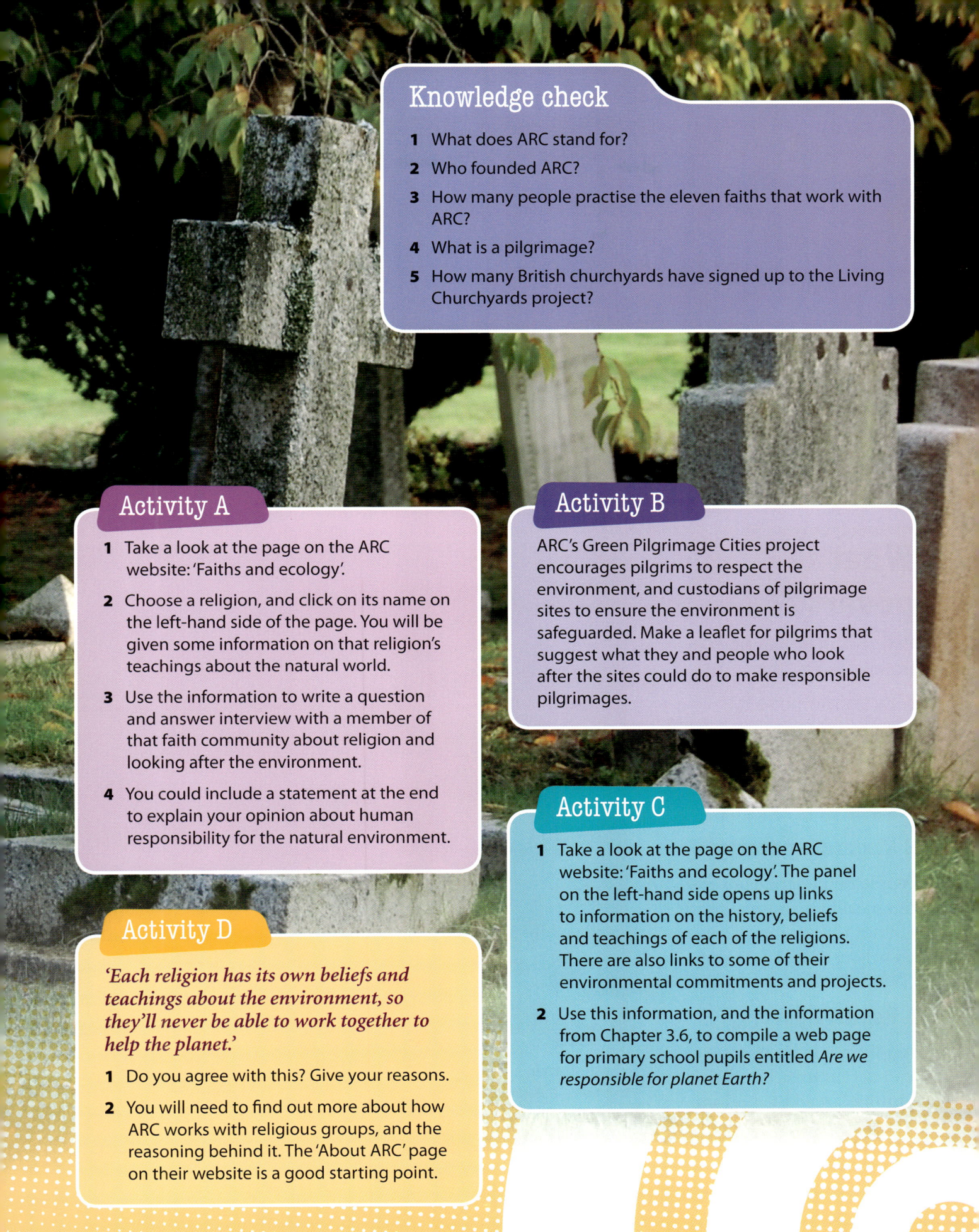

1. What does ARC stand for?
2. Who founded ARC?
3. How many people practise the eleven faiths that work with ARC?
4. What is a pilgrimage?
5. How many British churchyards have signed up to the Living Churchyards project?

Activity A

1. Take a look at the page on the ARC website: 'Faiths and ecology'.
2. Choose a religion, and click on its name on the left-hand side of the page. You will be given some information on that religion's teachings about the natural world.
3. Use the information to write a question and answer interview with a member of that faith community about religion and looking after the environment.
4. You could include a statement at the end to explain your opinion about human responsibility for the natural environment.

Activity B

ARC's Green Pilgrimage Cities project encourages pilgrims to respect the environment, and custodians of pilgrimage sites to ensure the environment is safeguarded. Make a leaflet for pilgrims that suggest what they and people who look after the sites could do to make responsible pilgrimages.

Activity C

1. Take a look at the page on the ARC website: 'Faiths and ecology'. The panel on the left-hand side opens up links to information on the history, beliefs and teachings of each of the religions. There are also links to some of their environmental commitments and projects.
2. Use this information, and the information from Chapter 3.6, to compile a web page for primary school pupils entitled *Are we responsible for planet Earth?*

Activity D

'Each religion has its own beliefs and teachings about the environment, so they'll never be able to work together to help the planet.'

1. Do you agree with this? Give your reasons.
2. You will need to find out more about how ARC works with religious groups, and the reasoning behind it. The 'About ARC' page on their website is a good starting point.

3.8 Are rich people responsible for the poor?

Learning objectives

You will …
- find out about degrees of poverty
- understand why religions promote relative poverty
- analyse ways in which religions put their beliefs about responsibility for the poor into action.

What is poverty?

Poverty can be described in three ways.

1 Extreme poverty

People in extreme poverty can barely meet their minimal needs for survival. They live on less than USD 1.25 a day.

2 Moderate poverty

People in moderate poverty can meet basic human needs, but not much more. They live on between USD 1.25 and USD 2.00 a day.

3 Relative poverty

People in relative poverty can lead decent lives, but their earnings are in the bottom 20 per cent of their region or country.

These women are queuing for food in Mogadishu, the capital of Somalia, in August 2011. They are standing beside a wall scarred with bullet holes. Somalia has been without a government since 1991, and a civil war has raged since then. As a result, the country is one of the poorest in the world. Life for ordinary people was made worse when drought struck the region. Food shortages and human rights abuses increased, affecting adults and children.

You don't have to be religious to believe that people who have money should use some of it to help the poor. The Universal Declaration of Human Rights says:
- All human beings are born free and equal in dignity and rights. They are endowed with reason and conscience and should act towards one another in a spirit of brotherhood. (Article 1)
- Everyone has the right to a standard of living adequate for the health and well-being of himself and of his family, including food, clothing, housing and medical care and necessary social services. (Article 25)

> *Poverty is pronounced deprivation in well-being, and comprises many dimensions. It includes low incomes and the inability to acquire the basic goods and services necessary for survival with dignity. Poverty also encompasses low levels of health and education, poor access to clean water and sanitation, inadequate physical security, lack of voice, and insufficient capacity and opportunity to better one's life.*
> (World Bank)

Religion and poverty

By and large, religions are not against people having money, or even having a lot of it. What they warn against is relying on money for happiness. For this reason, in many cultures, it is traditional for religious teachers to go without possessions and live simply.

Jesus taught that God would provide basic needs for anyone who followed him.

> *Do not worry about your life, what you will eat or drink … seek first [God's] kingdom and his righteousness, and all these things will be given to you as well.*
> (Matthew 6:25, 33)

So Jesus encouraged his followers to live simply as he did and not rely on possessions, but spiritual happiness.

> *One thing you lack … Go, sell everything you have and give [the money] to the poor, and you will have treasure in heaven. Then come, follow me.*
> (Mark 10:21)

The Buddha taught that people should not rely on luxuries to make them happy, but that they should not go without basic needs either. He called this the **Middle Way**.

> *There are two paths you must avoid. One is the path of luxury and material success. That path does not lead to true happiness. The other is the path of self-denial and starving yourself. That is a painful path, and it does not lead to true happiness.*
> (Dhammacakkappavattana Sutta)

So the Buddha encouraged his followers to lead a simple life, wearing cast-off clothes, begging for food and sleeping rough, just as he did.

> *A brother ... does this of his own free will because he knows that a life of faith will keep him away from temptations, will help him to avoid suffering, and will lead him towards **Enlightenment**.*
> (Vinaya, Mahavagga)

Still today, monks, nuns and **sadhus** (wandering holy men) give up their possessions to live simple, spiritual lives. Most religious people, of course, have jobs, families and homes. But they still believe that happiness does not lie in wealth.

This means that many religious people believe that, if they have more money than they need to live comfortably, they should use some of it to help people get out of extreme poverty.

Here are some ways that religious people help the poor.

Mother Teresa devoted her life to helping poor people in India.

- Muslims give a fixed portion of their wealth each year to help the poor. It is a religious duty, and is called **zakah**.

- A Christian nun, Mother Teresa of Calcutta, spent 45 years of her life helping people in India living in extreme poverty.

- Sikh ceremonies are always followed by **langar**, a free meal that can be taken by anyone, whether they are Sikh or not.

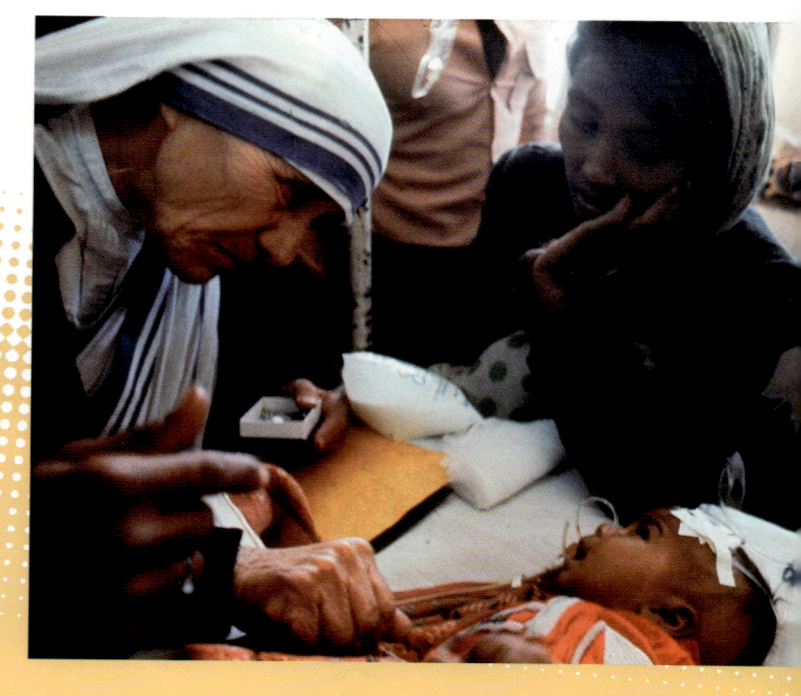

Knowledge check

1. What are the three forms of poverty?
2. According to the Universal Declaration of Human Rights, what sorts of things are important for a person's health and well-being?
3. Why did Jesus and the Buddha teach their followers to live in moderate poverty?
4. What is zakah?
5. Who was Mother Teresa of Calcutta?
6. What is langar?

Activity A

1. Conduct an imaginary interview with either Jesus or the Buddha to find out his views about having money and owning possessions.
2. Why did they live in moderate poverty?
3. Why did they suggest that their followers should live in moderate poverty?

Activity B

1. Write a report, or make a PowerPoint® presentation, on a religious charity that works to help people out of extreme poverty.
2. Find out about why they exist, how they operate, and give one or two examples of projects that they are or have been involved in.

Activity C

1. Read the World Bank's definition of poverty on page 87.
2. The World Bank says that absolute poverty often goes hand in hand with not having other human rights met. Conduct a small case study on one of the less economically developed countries (LEDCs) in the world, and produce a report on poverty and human rights.

Activity D

Religion is what keeps the poor man from murdering the rich.

Napoleon Bonaparte

1. What do you think Napoleon meant by this? Use examples from different religions to illustrate your answer.
2. Do you agree? Give reasons.

The big assignment

Task
To compile an information pack on religion and human rights.

Objectives
- To find out about the teachings and beliefs of one religion about human rights.
- To understand the issues that are associated with some human rights.
- To understand how religious teachings and beliefs about human rights can be put into practice.

Outcome
Your group is responsible for recruiting members to a religious human rights organisation. When people join, they are sent a welcoming pack that gives them information about the organisation, why it exists, and what it does. It is your team that puts the pack together.

Representatives pictured under the mural painted by Spanish artist Miquel Barcelo during a commemorative session at the assembly hall of the Human Rights Council to mark the 60th anniversary of the adoption of the Universal Declaration of Human Rights, December 2008.

Guidance

1. Work in groups of four or five. Each group in the class should represent a different religion.
2. Think of a name for your organisation.
3. Think of a slogan or strapline for your organisation that sums up what it is about.
4. Decide what your pack will contain. It could, for example, include:
   - an information leaflet about why your religion is concerned about human rights
   - postcards with quotations from your sacred texts or important leaders about human rights
   - an article about a champion of human rights from your religion
   - a leaflet advertising merchandise (T-shirts, caps, mugs, key rings, etc) with your organisation's slogan
   - case studies of the kinds of human rights abuses your organisation tries to highlight (e.g. prison reform, capital punishment, poverty).
5. Decide who in your group will be responsible for each part of the pack.
6. The completed pack should be able to fit into an A4 envelope.

Assessment

You will be assessed on:
- ✓ how you use specialist vocabulary
- ✓ your ability to describe and show understanding of religious sources, teachings and beliefs
- ✓ how well you show understanding of human rights issues
- ✓ your ability to describe and explain the impact of religion on people's lives.

Glossary

Abidharma texts that explain Buddhist teachings in detail

abiogenesis theory that life came from non-living materials

adhan Muslim call to prayer

adoration worship of God

amrit sugared water, symbolising eternal life (Sikhism)

artefact object used to help worship

atman the 'self' or **soul** of a person (Hinduism, Sikhism)

baptism ceremony to welcome a new member to the Christian community

biogenesis theory that life came from things that were already living

capital punishment death as a punishment for committing a crime

circumcise to remove the foreskin from the penis (Judaism, Islam)

death penalty see **capital punishment**

deterrence putting people off doing something

Divali festival celebrating good triumphing over evil (Hinduism, Sikhism)

Easter Festival celebrating the resurrection of Jesus (Christianity)

enlightenment understanding the truth about life

evolution theory that species develop from earlier forms of life

Five Ks five symbols of faith worn by Sikhs

fasting going without food for religious reasons

Guru Granth Sahib the holy book of Sikhism

Hadith sayings and advice from the Prophet Muhammad (Islam)

hanukiah eight-branched candlestick used at Hanukkah (Judaism)

Hanukkah festival celebrating the re-dedication of the Jewish Temple following victory over the Greeks (Judaism)

hijab head covering worn by some Muslim women to cover their hair and neck

jilbab long, loose coat worn by some Muslim women

kara bangle (one of the **Five Ks**) (Sikhism)

karma actions that have effects

langar free meal served after Sikh ceremonies; also the place where it is served

Lent 40 days leading up to **Easter** (Christianity)

menorah seven-branched candlestick (Judaism)

Middle way A way of life where a person does not rely on luxuries to make them happy, but does not go without basic needs either

moksha freedom from the cycle of birth and death (Hinduism)

mukti freedom from the cycle of birth and death (Sikhism)

niqab cloth worn by some Muslim women to cover the face, but not the eyes

pagoda building used for **veneration** (Buddhism)

Paschal candle candle lit in churches over **Easter** (Christianity)

pilgrimage journey made to a site of religious importance

Pope leader of the Roman Catholic Church (Christianity)

Qur'an the holy book of Islam

Ramadan ninth month of the Islamic year when Muslims fast

rebirth continuation of a person's **karma** in life after death (Buddhism, Hinduism, Sikhism)

reform to change the course of a person's life for the better

reincarnation the return of a **soul** to a new body after death

retribution punishing someone to get revenge

rite of passage stage of life when important changes take place

sadhu holy man (Buddhism, Hinduism)

samsara the world in which living things are born, live, die and are reborn (Buddhism, Hinduism, Sikhism)

sewa service to other people (Sikhism)

shalwar kameez baggy trousers and long, loose top worn by some Muslims

Shari'ah Islamic law

soul non-physical part of a person that gives them their individual identity

stupa dome-shaped structure used for **veneration** of the Buddha (Buddhism)

Talmud written teachings about the Jewish law

theistic evolution theory that evolution is a natural process in God's creation of the universe

Torah law; teaching; the first five books of the Bible (Judaism)

veneration showing deep respect for an object or person

yad pointer used for reading **Torah** scrolls

Yom Kippur Jewish day of fasting

zakah compulsory donation of money (one of the Five Pillars) (Islam)

Index

abiogenesis 35, 36
adulthood 19
animals
    animal rights 78–81
    and human beings 42–5
animo acids 36
the Arab Spring 76
ARC (Alliance of Religions and Conservation) 82–5
Aristotle 36
Aung San Suu Kyi 74

biogenesis 35, 36
birth 11, 18, 19
    ceremonies 20–2
the Buddha (Siddhartha Gautama) 9, 15, 37, 44
    enlightenment 12, 48, 49
    and the Middle Way 88
Buddhism
    the Abidharma 5
    and animal rights 80
    attaining enlightenment 48, 49
    and capital punishment 72
    death and rebirth 26, 27, 28, 54, 55
    defence of human rights 74
    and human beings 43, 44
    and marriage 25
    and punishment 68, 69
    stupas 27
    the Sutras 5
    Wesak 12
    worship 9

capital punishment 66, 70–3
celebration 11–13
chimpanzees 42, 43
Christianity
    and animal rights 78, 79
    baptism 21
    the Bible 5, 7, 37
    and capital punishment 72
    and death 26, 28, 52
    fasting 14, 15
    festivals 12
    and human beings 43
    and human rights 63, 64
        defence of 75
    Living Churchyards 84
    and marriage 24
    and poverty 87, 88
    and punishment 68
    and salvation 46

    worship 9
circumcision 21
creationism 36, 40

Dalai Lama 60
Darwin, Charles 38, 39
death 18, 19, 26–9
    beliefs about 50–1
    colours associated with 27
    funerals 26, 27
    monuments to the dead 27–8
    mourning 28–9
    and reincarnation 54–5
    and the soul 51, 52–3
death penalty 66, 70–3

Easter 12
environmentalism 82–5
evolution 38–41

Faith in Food 83
fasting 14–16
festivals 11–13
forests 84
funerals 26, 27

Gandhi, Mahatma 60, 75
Green Pilgrimage Cities 83

Hinduism
    and animal rights 80
    birth ceremonies 21
    and capital punishment 72
    death and rebirth 26, 28, 54, 55
    festivals 12, 13
    and human beings 43
    marriage 25
    moksha 47
    and punishment 68
    and the soul (atman) 53
    the Vedas 5
    worship 9
holy books 4–7
human beings 42–5
human rights 58–65
    defence of 74–7
    rights and responsibilities 58–9
    Universal Declaration of 59–60, 62, 72, 78, 87

independence in life 17–18
Islam

    and animal rights 78, 79
    and the Arab Spring 76
    birth ceremonies 21
    and capital punishment 73
    death
        and burial 26, 28, 29
        and the soul 53
    fasting 14, 15
    festivals 12
    the Hadith 5
    and human beings 43
    and human rights 61, 62, 63, 64
    and marriage 25
    and punishment 68, 69
    the Qur'an 5, 6, 37
    and salvation 47
    worship 9
    zakah 88

Jesus 12, 60, 87
journey of life 17–19
Judaism
    and animal rights 78, 79
    and capital punishment 72
    circumcision 21
    and death 26, 28, 52
    defence of human rights 76
    Hanukkah 13
    and human beings 43
    and marriage 24
    Pesach 12
    and punishment 68
    and salvation 47
    scriptures 5, 6
    Yom Kippur 15

karma 54, 55
King, Martin Luther 75

Lent 15
life, origins of 35–7

marriage 11, 18, 19, 23–5
    civil and religious ceremonies 23
Muhammad 5, 12, 21

Paschal candle 12
Pasteur, Louis 36
pilgrimages 83
the Pope 7
poverty 86–9
prisons 66
punishment 66–73
    death penalty 66, 70–3
    prisons 66
    purposes of 67
purpose of life 46–9

Ramadan 15
reincarnation 54–5
rites of passage 18–19

salvation 46–7
science and religion 32–4
Sikhism
    and animal rights 80
    birth ceremonies 21
    death and rebirth 26, 29, 47, 54, 55
    festivals 12, 13
    the Guru Granth Sahib 5, 7, 15, 21
    and human beings 43
    and human rights 63, 76
    and marriage 25
    and poverty 88
the soul 51, 52–3
    and reincarnation 54–5
spirituality, sense of 43, 46

Taj Mahal 27, 28
theistic evolution 39

the universe, origins of 32, 33

worship 8–10
    adoration and veneration 8, 9

Yom Kippur 15

The Publishers would like to thank the following for permission to reproduce copyright material:

Photo credits
p.5 © Nathan Benn/Ottochrome/Corbis; **p.6** *tr* © Abba Richman – Fotolia, *cl* © Stock Master – Fotolia; **p.7** *l* © Daniele Venturelli/Rex Features, *r* © NARINDER NANU/AFP/Getty Images; **p.11** *tl* © Mike Kemp/In Pictures/Corbis, *tr* © image100/SuperStock, *br* © Karin Hildebrand Lau – Fotolia; **p.12** *l* © Floris Leeuwenberg/Corbis, *tr* © Anna Bausova – Fotolia, *cr* © age fotostock/SuperStock, *br* © Photononstop/SuperStock; **p.13** © Dmitry Pistrov – Fotolia; **p.16** *all* © Steve Clarke; **p.20** © Glenda Powers – Fotolia; **p.26** © Brijesh Jaiswal/epa/Corbis; **p.27** *tl* © Konstantin Kalishko – Fotolia, *tr* © Shariff Che'Lah – Fotolia, *bl* © TMAX – Fotolia; **p.28** © Steve Clarke; **pp.30–31** *all* © Steve Clarke; **p.35** © Ivonne Wierink – Fotolia; **p.36** *t* © Argus – Fotolia, *b* © Blue Moon – Fotolia; **p.38** © So-Shan Au; **pp.40–41** © Bettmann/Corbis; **p.46** © 2010 The Art Archive/SuperStock; **p.48** © kelvinchuah – Fotolia; **p.51** © Leemage/Universal Images Group/Getty Images; **p.52** © Blue Lantern Studio/Corbis; **pp.56–57** © Mike Agliolo/Corbis; **p.60** © The Granger Collection, NYC/TopFoto; **p.67** © Steve Clarke; **p.70** © Image Source/Rex Features; **p.71** © Steve Clarke; **p.74** © CKN/Getty Images; **p.75** *t* © US National Archives, NWDNS-306-SSM-4C(51)13, *c* © EPA/Roberto Escobar/Corbis, *b* © SZ Photo/Scherl; **p.76** © Ann Hermes/The Christian Science Monitor via Getty Images; **p.79** *tl* © Josef Muellek – Fotolia, *tr* © Andreas Gradin – Fotolia, *b* © Bettmann/Corbis; **p.82** © CARL DE SOUZA/AFP/Getty Images; **p.83** *tr* © Eduard Zentshik – Fotolia, *cl* © alfrag – Fotolia; **p.84–85** © Steve Clarke; **p.86** © ROBERTO SCHMIDT/AFP/Getty Images; **p.88** © Sipa Press/Rex Features; **pp.90–91** © FABRICE COFFRINI/AFP/Getty Images.

Acknowledgements
Scripture quotations from The Holy Bible, New International Version Anglicised. Copyright © 1979, 1984 by Biblica, Inc. Used by permission of Hodder & Stoughton Publishers, a division of Hachette UK Ltd. All rights reserved. 'NIV' is a registered trademark of Biblica, Inc. UK trademark number 1448790; **p.34** Survey statistics from Caroline Lawes, Faith and Darwin: Harmony, Conflict, or Confusion? (Theos, 2009); **p.39** Quotation from Charles Darwin, *On the Origin of Species by Means of Natural Selection* (1859); **p.60** Second Article from Universal Declaration of Human Rights, adopted by the United Nations General Assembly (10 December 1948); **pp.82–85** Website information about ARC and its activities, reproduced by permission of the Alliance of Religions and Conservation (ARC), www.arcworld.org; **p.87** Quotation from 'What is Poverty and Why Measure It?', www.worldbank.org.

Every effort has been made to trace all copyright holders, but if any have been inadvertently overlooked the Publishers will be pleased to make the necessary arrangements at the first opportunity.